How do we draw the reality of women's experience in the history of the church in a way that doesn't simply reproduce its lines but reads between them and redraws them for the future? Mary-Elsie Wolfe shows how in this thin book, thick and rich with insights about the past, outlines of the present, and outfittings for the future.

—**Leonard Sweet**
Best-selling author, professor (Drew University, George Fox University),
and chief contributor to sermons.com

Mary-Elsie Wolfe weaves together a tapestry of everyday personal experiences, scholarly sources and devotional thoughts in this book about significant "moments" that women experienced with Jesus in the Gospel of John. She's not interested in debating the usual Pauline passages on the role of women in Christian communities; instead she invites the reader to watch, listen to and reflect on some very telling experiences and the underlying message that Jesus was giving about the place of women in his Kingdom.

—**Bishop Keith Elford**
Bishop of The Free Methodist Church in Canada (1997 to 2017),
executive committee member of the Free Methodist World Conference

Mary-Elsie Wolfe draws us into the stories of women in the New Testament who have fully embraced their calling and illustrates the lessons learned through her own life experiences. The invitation is to see with new eyes how Jesus and the early Church broke with cultural norms to include women and then to look beyond the restrictions of our own culture in order to participate in what God is birthing in the church today.

—**Lynn Smith**
Former VP of Student Development/Dean of Students, Tyndale University
College and Seminary; author of **Gender or Giftedness** *and* **Mentoring: Leaving a**
Legacy; *founding member of NextLEVEL Leadership*

Think of Christianity as a set of doctrines to believe or rules to observe? Then this book is for you. Wolfe makes clear, Christ is not out to make us dutiful servants but to win our hearts with his all-embracing love. Having Christ formed in us is what our souls hunger for. Mary-Elsie makes clear that no matter who we are, "our season of life is no barrier to having Christ formed in us."

—**Elisabeth Natividad**
Lead Pastor, Grace Methodist Church

This is the best book I have read on the topic of leadership from the perspective of a coaching relationship. As a professional executive leadership coach, I find Mary-Elsie's treatment of leadership refreshing as well as motivational. She deals with women and men in leadership in a fair and balanced way. Her thoughts about followership are quite insightful for both genders. If you want to learn more about leadership, become renewed in your leadership or have questions about women in leadership, this is a must-read book.

—Patrick Lattore, PhD
President of PAL~Leadership (an executive coaching company),
former associate provost and faculty member teaching leadership
at Fuller Theological Seminary

MARY-ELSIE WOLFE

BECOMING HIS STORY

INSPIRING WOMEN TO LEADERSHIP

Becoming His Story: Inspiring Women to Leadership
Copyright ©2017 Mary-Elsie Wolfe
All rights reserved
Printed in Canada
ISBN 978-1-927355-52-7 (soft cover)
ISBN 978-1-927355-53-4 EPUB

Published by:
Castle Quay Books
Burlington, Ontario
Tel: (416) 573-3249
E-mail: info@castlequaybooks.com   www.castlequaybooks.com

Edited by Marina Hofman Willard
Cover and interior design by Burst Impressions
Printed at Essence Printing, Belleville, Ontario

Library and Archives Canada Cataloguing in Publication

Wolfe, Mary-Elsie, author
    Becoming his story : inspiring women to leadership / Mary-Elsie Wolfe.

ISBN 978-1-927355-52-7 (softcover)

    1. Christian women--Religious life. 2. Leadership--Religious aspects--Christianity. 3. Leadership in women. 4. Christian life. I. Title.

BV4527.W64 2017   248.8'43   C2017-901120-0

CASTLE QUAY BOOKS

DEDICATION

TO ELIZABETH, ABBY, ELIANA AND AMY—MY BEAUTIFUL NIECES AND DAUGHTERS. May your lives be a tapestry of grace, beauty and the fruit of the Spirit, leading others to better places, propelled by the love of God, with full engagement of the gifts and talents that you offer the world! And to Alex, Patrick, Fletcher, Braden and Gregory, may you foster a world that enjoys the freedom of all people and sees your dreams through God's lens of hope. To all of you, dream big—in partnership with the God who is so much bigger!

CONTENTS

ACKNOWLEDGEMENTS   9
PREFACE   11

SECTION ONE
TO LEARN FROM JESUS

CHAPTER 1   17
MY STORY

CHAPTER 2   19
WORLDVIEW AND CULTURAL LENS

CHAPTER 3   22
THE TRUTH ABOUT WOMEN

CHAPTER 4   25
THE WOMEN IN JOHN:
JESUS ASPIRES TO GREAT THINGS FOR WOMEN

CHAPTER 5   27
CONTEXT AND HISTORY

CHAPTER 6   32
MARY MODELS DISCIPLESHIP 101

CHAPTER 7   39
A FEMALE APOSTLE IS THE FIRST EVANGELIST

CHAPTER 8   50
MARTHA: CONVICTING FAITH LEADS TO A DEMONSTRATION
OF THE POWER OF GOD

CHAPTER 9   59
MARY (SISTER OF MARTHA AND LAZARUS):
DEMONSTRATES COSTLY FOLLOWERSHIP AND PASSIONATE FAITH
THROUGH HER LOVE AND DEVOTION TO JESUS

CHAPTER 10   66
WOMEN AT THE CROSS:
RESOLUTELY LOYAL AND UNWAVERING UNTIL THE END;
FIRST TO HEAR OF MISSION COMPLETION

CHAPTER 11:   70
MARY OF BETHANY: THE UNRELENTING LEADER

SECTION TWO
TO LIVE LIKE JESUS

CHAPTER 12   77
WOMEN LEAD THE WAY, ENLARGING OUR VIEW BY FOLLOWING

CHAPTER 13   81
WOMEN LEADING IN THE CHURCH MOVE US CLOSER TO THE FULLNESS
OF GOD'S COMPLETED WORK

CHAPTER 14   87
THE PROMINENCE OF WOMEN IN THE EARLY CHURCH

SECTION THREE
TO LEAD LIKE JESUS

CHAPTER 15   97
JESUS DEFINES LEADERSHIP:
LEADERSHIP THEORY DRAWS FROM JESUS

CHAPTER 16   105
THE LOVE OF GOD IS THE FOUNDATION OF CHRISTIAN LEADERSHIP

CHAPTER 17   111
GIVING POWER AWAY IN ORDER TO FOSTER AND REALIZE VISION

CHAPTER 18   114
DISCERNING THE BIRTH OF NEW VISION FOR THE CHURCH:
A CAUSE TO RECOMMIT TO WOMEN IN LEADERSHIP

CHAPTER 19   128
LEADERS FOLLOW JESUS, THEN INVEST IN THE MAKING OF OTHER LEADERS

CHAPTER 20   130
LEARNING FROM JESUS, LIVING LIKE JESUS, LEADING LIKE JESUS:
BECOMING THE BEST STORY EVER

ACKNOWLEDGEMENTS

COPIOUS THANKS TO MY FAMILY, EXTENDED FAMILY AND FRIENDS WHO HAVE through the years encouraged me to finish this project! To my mom, dad, siblings and daughters for cheering me on in life and loving me. Special thanks to Kathleen Fletcher for your constructive feedback and hours of proofreading. Thanks to Marina Hofman Willard for guiding this process with dedication and patience—especially with footnotes—and for your pointed comments that very much improved the end product. Thanks to my husband, Grant, for walking this journey with me and encouraging my dreams. Mostly, thanks to Jesus, who leads my way, infuses in me undying hope and models for me what love looks like!

PREFACE

WHAT IF THERE *WAS* SOMETHING NEW UNDER THE SUN? WHAT IF WE ARE participating in changes that will someday define this period as a new era? Some would say we live in such a time. Certainly, church as we know it in the Western world is changing. I say Western world because many parts of Christendom around the world are flourishing, but change could certainly be reflected in the church worldwide.

Many Christian leaders are reassessing how Jesus understood church, how the early worshipers congregated, how we arrived at the forms of church we now attend. As leaders, men and women, we want to rise up to that challenge and discern what God is doing among us. In some traditions, some circles and some theological camps, women aren't always encouraged to fully participate. This book seeks to inspire women to fully engage in that call—and to inspire men to challenge the women in their lives to rise up to meet God's mission.

God could more expediently enflame a bush, give repeated Damascus-road experiences, or keep fleece dry amidst the dew. Instead, he chooses to share the journey in partnership with us. Even with our many foibles and imperfections and our inability to fully listen or understand, God patiently guides us along in his mission. As *our* hearts grow to understand more fully *his* heart, we also share in his joy. The Psalmist glimpses the fullness of this joy, reminding us that a single day in God's presence is better than a thousand elsewhere (Psalm 84:10). God calls us to a lifetime of such days in his joyful presence. Every day we have the opportunity to experience God's deep call and presence in new ways. As the people of God, we embark on that journey. We allow God's Spirit to work in us. We learn from Jesus. We live more like Jesus. We lead like Jesus. All as his Spirit indwells ours. As we allow God's story to *live* in our story, we are in a sense *becoming his story*. Jesus says, "remain in me, and I will remain in you" (John 15:4). The more we do, the more we have opportunity to live in the abundance to which God calls us (John 10:10).

That is not to say that we don't routinely face challenges in our daily life—anxieties about family and friends, health challenges, financial irregularities, physical or natural tragedies, and even the minutia of daily routine and rituals. But how we invite God into those challenges can encourage us to a deeper understanding and revelation of his love. Furthermore, it can rewrite our story as one of transformation, inspiration, and adventure—as God's story increasingly becomes part of ours.

In the 1980s teen-slacker classic *Ferris Bueller's Day Off*, the title character makes a profound statement: "Life moves pretty fast. [If] you don't stop and look around once in a while, you could miss it." As the rock group the Rolling Stones found out since popularizing the song *Time Is on Our Side* 40 years ago, life moves quickly. I'm not sure most of us grasp life's speed until we are well into our 30s. I recall a conversation with my paternal grandmother when I was about 11—words that meant very little to me then. "You won't understand this now," she said, "but life is much shorter than you think." Not that I've reached the age when she transferred this wisdom, but I *get* it. I'm now convinced that time moves more quickly every year that I live.

But take comfort. If you live in partnership with the living God, he promises to satisfy you "with good as long as you live," even renewing your youth (Psalm 103:5 NRSV). That means that even if you feel that you have wasted time and it's just too late, with God there is always hope. As long as he keeps us on this earth, we are invited to this privileged partnership. We are invited to allow his story to grow into ours.

If you feel that you are someone who has wasted time, consider St. Augustine. For over 30 years, he overtly resisted God's grace, while his praying mother anticipated his eventual divine encounter. Today, he is considered one of the most-noted theological influences of Western theology among our Christian Fathers and Mothers. The apostle Paul was personally responsible for persecuting Christians and supported the stoning of Stephen (Acts 8:1). Paul admitted as much in his letter to the Galatians, saying that he was "violently persecuting the church of God and was trying to destroy it" (Gal. 1:13 NRSV). One might think that with his past, he would constantly be feeling regret and remorse, but his words to the Philippians are promising for all of us: "*forgetting* what lies behind and *straining* forward to what lies ahead" (Phil. 3:13 NRSV, emphasis added).

What must have thrilled Paul even more was that his education, background, and life experiences all seemed to have moulded together so that his new life in Jesus became beautiful pottery. God used Paul's abilities and experiences for his greater purposes. Paul lived in full partnership with God. We are invited to do the same. Wherever you are in your journey of faith, in your season of life, or in living out God's call, it is my hope that reading *Becoming His Story* will be a journey of inspiration.

This book will be divided into three sections: To Learn from Jesus; To Live Like Jesus; To Lead Like Jesus. Section 1 is about call and inspiration: to learn from Jesus. The discussion is guided by the Gospel of John, as in it, more so than the other Gospels, we are invited to observe how Jesus interacts with women.[1] One writer says, "Jesus' approach to women was in such contrast to that of his culture that we can assume a deliberate modeling of a new way of relating to women."[2]

We are challenged to consider our formative, environmental, and cultural biases that hinder our full view when reading about the time of Jesus. In these stories, women were called personally by Jesus. How these women responded and interacted with Jesus gives us great insight into what Jesus aspires to for women. These portraits of Jesus and women offer deep theological significance.

The culture at Christ's time was influenced by Roman, Greek, Qumranic, and ancient Jewish thinking. Each of these groups held distinct yet somewhat similar perspectives on women, adapting to new opportunities for female leadership differently. But as Jesus meets these women in John, he seems determined not to be limited by cultural norms.

Because of the boldness of Jesus' mother Mary, we witness Jesus' first miracle and learn about discipleship. Thanks to an unknown Samaritan woman, we get a preview of Jesus' mission and then her personal commissioning to share about whom she encountered. In Martha, we have a powerful profession of faith articulating the identity of Jesus, followed by actions that convey her convictions about Jesus. When Mary the sister of Martha and Lazarus anoints the feet of Jesus with perfume, we learn about costly followership. With the women at the cross in the final hours of Jesus' death, we learn about being resolutely loyal and unwavering until the very end. We also see God including those who were within that close range in his declaration of the completion of his mission. From that we learn how abiding with Jesus entitles us to have firsthand communication about his work in the world.

And finally, thanks to the example of Mary of Bethany at the tomb, we have the example of an unrelenting leader, the one who receives the first communication after the resurrection because of her relentless pursuit of Christ.

Section 2 begins with women who led in how to follow Jesus. In Romans 16, we see that women are in leadership positions alongside of Paul. We see examples in Acts 21 of women teaching and prophesying.

The early church that took form after the resurrection of Jesus existed between the "the already and the not yet." Victory over death had been accomplished, but the full

---

[1] For a more exhaustive study on women in the Bible, see Cynthia Long Westfall, *Paul and Gender: Reclaiming the Apostle's Vision for Men and Women in Christ* (Grand Rapids: Baker Academic, 2016).

[2] Karen Heidebrecht Thiessen, "Jesus and Women in the Gospel of John," *Direction* 19, no. 2 (Fall 1990): 53.

consummation of that victory was still to come. But living toward that consummation seemed natural.

Men and women are equally called to serve as leaders. Unfortunately, church history and society have not always reflected that. Still today, in some denominational traditions, women are faced with obstacles to leadership. For new generations of women, who anticipate the world as their oyster, it seems odd and inconsistent to discover that cultural traditions or misperceptions will limit their opportunities within the church as part of the priesthood of believers. This results in competent, gifted women withholding their areas of giftedness in view of a perceived but misaligned obedience to Scripture. Or, talented, capable women might disregard Christianity altogether as the misconceptions in some churches taint their perceptions of following Jesus. Other women might have been raised in traditions that have excluded them from their true calling in the church.

Section 3 is about leading like Jesus. Jesus defines leadership. Much of leadership theory seems to draw from Jesus. The difference with Christian leadership is that it begins with our love for God—which is in fact the foundational premise for Christian leaders. Following the example of Jesus, leaders give power away as they discern vision and then see it realized. The same observational, prayerful discernment is necessary for the church to participate in what God is doing in the world. If we are in fact in a time of transition as a Christian movement, recommitting women to leadership will better position us to receive the full potential of God's blessing for the church. Jesus invites followership to replicate his investment in others and multiply leadership. Leaders follow Jesus and then invest in the making of other leaders.

Regardless of your personal history, this book is for you. May you be inspired toward greater male/female leadership! As you learn, live and lead, experience how you can increasingly allow God's story to live in yours—*becoming his story*.

SECTION ONE

TO LEARN FROM JESUS

Anyone who wanders away from this teaching
has no relationship with God. But anyone who
remains in the teaching of Christ has a
relationship with both the Father
and the Son.

(2 John 9)

CHAPTER 1
MY STORY

AS A FAIRLY NEW BELIEVER I WOULD SAY, "I JUST WANT TO FOLLOW JESUS." ONE morning while jogging, I reflected aloud to a friend on an upcoming course paper that I was assigned. As each step carried the weight of my stride, I verbally scrolled through my options of possible topics, pausing when I got to the role of women in the Gospel of John. My friend interjected, "I think that's what you should do!"

I reflected on this. I sensed that my life had and would continue to have calls of leadership, but for whatever reason, I resisted. It would have been irresponsible of me not to acknowledge that I was "surrounded by...a cloud of witnesses" who could give me insight via my research into the subject (Heb. 12:1 NRSV).

Until that point, I had no need to research the topic. I was raised Roman Catholic, where the ordination of women certainly wasn't an option. In addition, I was influenced by conservative Protestant teaching. I even recall my reaction when, at a cross-denominational Bible study in downtown Ottawa, I met a woman who announced that she had just quit her job and enrolled in seminary in Toronto. The voice in my head said, *Why would a woman go to seminary?*

A few weeks after this encounter, my employer announced a restructuring of its Ottawa office. It seemed like a perfect moment to seize; within weeks, I too was on my way to Tyndale Seminary (then Ontario Theological Seminary).

Well into earning my degree, I remained content to study about God, his relationship with his world and his plan for keeping relationship with us. Here I was in seminary, seeking to delve into God's Word as it pertained to me and my relationship with God and yet disregarding my gender—even at the same time as the issue of gender was sometimes a hot issue in the church and at seminary. By God's very gentle prodding, I realized I needed to look honestly at how Jesus interacted with women. I did so, on my knees, with tears of humility, before the God I follow. Thus began an intentional review of women in the Gospel of John, leading me to deepen my journey to *Becoming His Story.*

CHAPTER 2

WORLDVIEW AND CULTURAL LENS

JESUS SAID,

> "I will ask the Father, and He will give you another Helper, that He may be with you forever; that is the Spirit of truth, whom the world cannot receive, because it does not see Him or know Him, but you know Him because He abides with you and will be in you." (John 14:16–17 NASB)

> "When the Spirit of truth comes, he will guide you into all truth. He will not speak on his own but will tell you what he has heard. He will tell you about the future." (John 16:13)

It would seem that any study on which we embark benefits by our recognition that we have formative, environmental, and cultural biases that might hinder our view. We are guided closer to truth when we start recognizing that our preconceived notions can hinder our ability to see clearly. Once we identify what those notions might be, we are better able to avoid looking for those details that only confirm our existing understanding. The goal is not to filter out that which may give clarity, even if it opposes our way of understanding. Certainly with political views, in cultural studies, and in personal relationships, it is a challenge to allow ourselves to be enlightened by new information that starts from an opposing or different view than ours. Our lens can be limited.

That is also the case when looking at the Bible. Imposing our cultural or formative or generational view on what we read can hinder our view. Therefore, we need to be stretched to step ourselves, as much as possible, into the biblical context and worldview in which we are reading. New Testament scholars, historians, and archaeologists help us do that. I look at the Gospel of John from that context.

Of the four Gospels (Matthew, Mark, Luke and John), the Gospel of John stands alone in many ways. It was written later—near the end of the first century. The other three evangelists wrote somewhere between AD 30 and 70.

Particular to the beloved disciple, as John describes himself, is what he highlights about how Jesus interacts with women.[1] John breathes fresh spiritual depth about how Jesus interacts with women.

Whether you have never read the Gospel of John or have read it over many times, I invite you to read it with fresh eyes. Listen to what the Holy Spirit may be telling you as you imagine yourself hearing and watching Jesus. I challenge you to consider whatever preconceptions might hinder you from doing that and omit whatever filters will keep you from seeing clearly. It is challenging, but doable.

Let me share a personal story. I remember as a newlywed booking our first flight to Regina. My husband, Grant, and I had planned on visiting his mom for a week. He was in the midst of trying to meet a deadline, and I had been busily consumed with finishing work assignments before our departure. With our luggage in hand, we walked through the express ticket booth, pressing *enter* at cue for our destination. We got on the plane in comfort, feeling all was well with the world!

As our plane began to descend, the captain's voice interrupted my movie, giving me the temperature for Saskatoon! "Saskatoon?" I smiled to myself. "He must be someone from Ontario mixing up the two major cities in Saskatchewan." We were on our way to Regina, not Saskatoon. As we deplaned and walked toward the arrivals lounge, my husband, who had lived in both Regina and Saskatoon, commented, "They must be making renovations to the Regina airport. This is quite nice." We walked a bit farther before he added, this time with a tone of suspicion and almost accusation, "This airport looks distinctly like the Saskatoon airport!" Suddenly, he stopped at one of the advertisement posters encased in glass and said very soberly, "We are in Saskatoon!" I paused with concern, feeling pretty stupid since I was the one who had booked the tickets!

We had indeed landed in Saskatoon—not Regina! But until that very moment, we were reading all the circumstances around us through the eyes of our preconceived notions. I *thought* that I had booked our tickets for Regina and had no reason to think otherwise. While many signs could have revealed the truth about our destination, I was blinded by my preconceptions. Truth was veiled and distorted. Even though everything around me indicated we were not in the Saskatoon airport,

---

[1] While some scholars have suggested that the book was authored by disciples of John, I follow the traditional view of its author being John.

I was oblivious—blind to what was right in front of me. Unless we are aware of what blinds our view, we will miss the full benefit of a particular experience or insight.

Let the Holy Spirit, who leads you into all truth, help you become aware of any preconceived notions that may prevent you from seeing from God's eyes. Whether you are a man or woman seeking to inspire others, or for that matter to be inspired yourself, take a moment to ask the Holy Spirit to lead you into all truth. Invite the Holy Spirit into your story.

CHAPTER 3
THE TRUTH ABOUT WOMEN

"DID YOU WASH YOUR HANDS?"

"Yes, Mom," she said with a slight hesitation in her voice.

"You did?" I inquired.

"Yes, Mom, I did." This time, a little emphatic.

Mentally calculating the time that would be required to actually go the bathroom, turn on the tap, pump the soap dispenser, turn off the water, and reach over for a hand towel, I asked again, "Are you sure you washed your hands with soap?"

"Yes, Mom, I did!" She stepped back, clearly defining her personal space far away from mine.

"Here, let me smell them," I persisted. She opened her craft-filled hands, marked with the evidence of glue-flaked fingertips, sheepishly waiting for me to smell her hands. As I paused and looked into her eyes, I said with encouragement, "Maybe you should wash them again."

It's difficult in a world of quasi-truth to believe that truth actually exists. In fact, the task of discerning truth can be daunting in the midst of opinion pieces, news articles, and the views of different spokespeople with agendas. But Jesus claims truth, even when our culture denies it. In our current world, circumstances and situations can determine the heart of most matters.

I recall hearing an interview with legendary '70s–'80s artist Lionel Ritchie. The interviewer asked him to explain what he meant by the lyrics of his song "My Heart Is Aching Just for You." He stated that it was written for all of us—for himself. He recalled how, when he was a child, right and wrong were black and white. He added, "In our current age, everything is circumstantial and grey...and everyone now uses God for their own purposes."

Lionel Ritchie may not have realized that he was actually stating simply what philosophers have been observing for years. People who write about the change of eras say that the era in which we currently live (commonly called postmodern— the time that follows the modern era) characterizes truth as fabrication. In other words, people are free to believe in whatever *truth* they deem fits their situation and circumstance. We ask them, "How is it working for you?" If it is working, then we accept it as *their* personal truth.

The problem with this conclusion is that Jesus claims truth in the Gospel of John, even referring to himself as *being* the truth. It is in fact a book of God's truth. Believers in God are invited to meet the source of truth in John. Through John's message, we see women of different generations invited by Jesus personally to see his arms out-stretched with a welcoming presence to meet their call. Angela Ravin-Anderson writes,

> Because Jesus provided no explicit teaching with regard to the roles of women in ministry, his position on the topic can best be ascertained by observing his actions and listening to his words as he interacts with the women in his world.[2]

It is like Jesus is saying that although there might be baggage from misunder-standings, misguided teaching, false assumptions, or even excuses in the name of obedience, "You should open your eyes to see how I interacted with women while here on earth."

I remember a very academically gifted man in seminary discussing the issue of God's call to women. While we agreed on many issues, he concluded that, still, women should not be given positions of leadership in the church; nor should they teach men. I believe that an honest look at Jesus disputes that claim.

I fear that any Christian church still not operating in light of Jesus' actions toward women will miss out.

Some of us are in our bubbles, oblivious to the fact that Christian women around the world face inadequate teaching on this issue. Cultures and church contexts read into their own bias that Jesus called 12 *male* disciples. Therefore, only men should be called as leaders.

Church history reveals differently. It was commonly understood in the 18th and 19th centuries that the early church was egalitarian and only "supplanted to hierarchical leadership in the second century."[3] Some would call it even a truism that Pauline churches and some parts of the Jesus movement in Galilee were egalitarian.[4]

---

[2] Angela Ravin-Anderson, "They Had Followed Him from Galilee: The Female Disciples," *Priscilla Papers* 28, no. 2 (Spring 2014).

[3] Mary Ann Beavis, "Christian Origins, Egalitarianism, and Utopia," *Journal of Feminist Studies in Religion* 23, no. 2 (2007): 37.

[4] Beavis, "Christian Origins, Egalitarianism, and Utopia," 36.

But while some researchers and academics have come to these conclusions, this insight isn't always translated into common knowledge. This is one reason why I wrote this book.

Some churches, even in the Western world, retain a bias against women. Very recently I sat in a church as a visitor where the chair of the pastoral search committee got up and emphatically, and repeatedly, talked about finding a godly *man* to hold the position of pastor in that church.

Where we show favour to one gender over another, thereby impeding a call of Jesus, we will be held accountable.

We will be held accountable for how that impediment has prevented us from more fully experiencing God's kingdom here on earth—more fully being part of his story. Jesus prayed for God's kingdom to come!

CHAPTER 4

THE WOMEN IN JOHN:
JESUS ASPIRES TO GREAT THINGS FOR WOMEN

WOMEN IN THE GOSPEL OF JOHN ARE MAIN CHARACTERS IN SCENES THAT CARRY deep theological significance. How these women responded and interacted with Jesus gives us great insight into what Jesus aspires to for women.

The Gospels can best be described as portraits of Jesus. In featuring the Gospel of John, we are seeing a portrait. Karen Thiessen writes,

We are left with an implicit commentary by John, who portrays women as active, innovative ministers of the kingdom...the Johannine Jesus affirms them in roles that were unusual and often unacceptable within that culture. Jesus' approach to women was in such contrast to that of his culture that we can assume a deliberate modeling of a new way of relating to women.[5]

That's what we understand from the Gospel of John. But still, well-respected pastors and theologians can think otherwise.

I remember meeting such a pastor and later conveying this encounter to my fiancé. I happened to mention that this pastor didn't believe women should be in ministry—especially in the pulpit.

With honest and refreshing inquisitiveness, and perhaps a sense of mischief, as if God were using the moment to confirm that Grant was the man for me, my fiancé replied, "Doesn't he read the Bible?"

I believe that the Bible makes the call and ministry of women very clear. But I also believe that we—all men and women—are to serve in humility. That is, never should it be about holding power or position over the other. Still today, there are teachers

---

[5] Thiessen, "Jesus and Women," 53.

and commentaries that seem to be saying something like God made men first; therefore women can't lead men. Jesus never fought for power. In fact, it was by being humbled that Christ was exalted. Serving Jesus is not a battle for authority or one-upmanship but rather a humble attitude of servanthood.

Furthermore, it is not a right for people to claim their own calling—especially when it comes to the ministry of God's Word. A person's call to ministry shouldn't be about pushing an agenda, because everyone has equal access to God's call. It is a privilege granted by God himself. The church simply recognizes and affirms this divine call.

We have an invitation in the Gospel of John. We are invited to see women as key players dancing in theological discourse with the master of teachers himself—Jesus. In the Gospel of John, women are reflective, responsive, and even commissioned by Jesus himself to teach others. Their actions are decisive. Their reflections are challenging. Their witness reflects on their calling, and there is a singleness of purpose in their response to Jesus.

Men and women today continue to be called to acquaint themselves with Jesus. Still, Jesus calls women individually and uniquely to use their gifts and passions for great purposes. Even now, God is calling men and women around the world to convey their experiences from their own faith journey for the encouragement of others. Jesus is calling all of us as he did Martha, the Samaritan woman, Mary Magdalene, Mary of Bethany—as we explore through this book. He has called people throughout Christian history to respond to him according to his call. And like these other women through history, abiding with him in his call will bring us significance and meaning unlike anything else. It will bring us into his story.

CHAPTER 5
CONTEXT AND HISTORY

WHEN I WAS ON THE ELLIPTICAL TRAINER ONE MORNING, I FOUND MYSELF WATCHING reruns of an old program called *All in the Family*. It would be an understatement to suggest that the main character, Archie, has issues. He is insensitive to U.S. minorities, like African Americans and Hispanics, and buys into any stereotypes society might give them.

One day, Archie is stuck on an elevator with a very pregnant Hispanic woman, her very rich, accomplished African American husband, and a claustrophobic white woman who is socially challenged. The inevitable happens. The pregnant woman goes into labour. Everyone but Archie huddles together to assist in the birth, while Archie squirms in the corner, wincing at each scream and each carefully narrated description that the others are only too pleased to share with him.

When rescued, Archie retells the story with himself as the hero—taking all the credit for the baby's birth and, by his account, being the only one who displayed courage and strength to get the others through the ordeal—when, in fact, he was the only one who panicked. The people who lived through the incident would have known that Archie's version was contrived. Probably the people who knew Archie well also would have suspected that his story was misleading. That is because his words and description didn't tell the whole story.

Knowing about Archie's hang-ups and misperceptions connects us to his personal history. We better understand the scenario and what actually happened by better knowing Archie. Context is explained by Archie's character.

Similarly, we understand biblical context by better knowing the character of Jesus. As we grow in our relationship with Jesus, by his own revelation, we better understand his teaching and those who followed him.

Likewise, knowing biblical culture also helps us understand the context of a biblical text. What might be easily understood by one generation or culture might be totally misunderstood by another. Misunderstanding can lead to us feeling smug and labelling or considering what we don't understand as stupid. Take for example an article published in *The Globe and Mail* called "Britain's Stupidest Statutes."[6]

In this article, a number of outdated laws are listed. What we need to keep in mind is that these laws at one time responded to real needs. They were laws that probably reacted to real situations. For laws to pass in any culture or context, real people had to spend time thinking about them. But pulled out of context and landing within the context of our 21st century worldview, they may seem nothing less than stupid!

Here are some examples that are listed:

• It is an act of treason to place a postage stamp bearing the British monarch upside down.
• In Liverpool, it is illegal for a woman to be topless, unless she is a clerk in a tropical fish store.
• A pregnant woman can legally relieve herself anywhere she wants, including in a policeman's helmet.
• Mince pies cannot be eaten on Christmas Day.

And the number one dumbest of dumb statutes in Britain is…

• It is illegal to die in the Houses of Parliament.

We read these laws and find them funny, realizing that to each piece of legislation there is history that no longer connects to us. Understanding each of these statutes is possible only when we have the benefit of the fuller context and history. As we discussed how knowing a person can define context, so too can history complete the story. That's what we want to keep in mind when we look at the Bible.

God divinely inspired 66 different books through different people at different points in history for different reasons. Understanding how women were treated and viewed in the time of Jesus is important to our better understanding the books that were written after his having been here.

The culture at Christ's time was influenced by Roman, Greek, Qumranic, and ancient Jewish thinking. Each of these groups held distinct yet somewhat similar perspectives on women. Perhaps this is why we see different communities of early Christian faith adapting to new opportunities for female leadership differently. Scholar

---

[6] Philip Jackman, "Britain's Stupidest Statutes," *The Globe and Mail*, November 7, 2007, accessed January 14, 2017, http://www.theglobeandmail.com/news/world/britains-stupidest-statutes/article1089086/.

Susan Hylen makes this point well as she recognizes women's leadership within the early church as a reality but demonstrates how communities adapted for that change based on respective gender bias.[7] Here are some examples of how each group reflected gender bias by community.

Greek women were considered a means of creating healthy citizens.[8] In the Greco-Roman world, women could not sign or pay for another's debt. Women who worked alongside their husbands might be trained as skilled tradespeople. More privileged women might have published poetry, studied philosophy, or painted, but typically under the direction of their husband.[9] If there were evening dinner events, women would not participate in cases where there were men unrelated to them present.[10] Women were prevented from holding political office and serving in the military.

The Roman view was that women were generally inferior[11] and were to remain under the dominance of their husbands.[12]

In Greco-Roman society, legislating and enforcing the "proper" behaviour of women was a major concern for authorities because they believed that disorder in the household had seditious ramifications for the welfare of the empire.[13]

In wealthy homes, women might have owned property and slaves and were tasked to run operations for the familial home.[14] Women were allowed to be present for evening parties, but the guests were primarily male and the parties were focused around political kibitzing.[15] Both men and women could be priests, provided the cult's beliefs allowed it,[16] but "cults and sects were often attacked because of the wild behaviour of the women participants."[17]

So with this backdrop, "there were women who gravitated to the study of Scripture and formulation of theology." This usually happened in wealthy matrons'

---

[7] Susan Hylen, *A Modest Apostle: Thecla and the History of Women in the Early Church* (Oxford: Oxford University Press, 2015).

[8] Mary Evans, *Woman in the Bible* (Devon: Paternoster Press, 1983), 40.

[9] Lynn Cohick, "Women, Children, and Families in the Roman World," in *The World of the New Testament: Cultural, Social, and Historical Contexts*, eds. Joel Green and Lee Martin McDonald (Grand Rapids: Baker Academic, 2013), 183.

[10] Cohick, "Women, Children, and Families," 180.

[11] Westfall, *Paul and Gender*, 14.

[12] Evans, *Woman in the Bible*, 40.

[13] Westfall, *Paul and Gender*, 13.

[14] Cohick, "Women, Children, and Families," 183.

[15] Cohick, "Women, Children, and Families," 180.

[16] Cohick, "Women, Children, and Families," 181.

[17] Westfall, *Paul and Gender*, 13.

homes, and later less formal monastic communities developed.[18] Their stories—that is the early church mothers who contributed to formational theology—haven't been well documented. Tucker professes that is because theologians from Augustine to Aquinas to Luther and Wesley and Barth were men. She adds that a fitting sign on their clubhouse door could have read "No Daughters of Eve Allowed," arguing that daughters of Eve were the ones tempted by Satan first and who fell into sin.

In the Talmud, a woman is described as "a picture full of filth with its mouth full of blood."[19]

In regards to marriage, it is believed that some Jews had two or more wives. Women were only to be sexually intimate with their husbands; however, men were only considered adulterers if they had sexual relations with another man's wife.[20]

Finally, the Qumran people had a view of women that was considered more narrow and restrictive to women's rights than that of the Jews.[21]

Since Jesus was a Jew, the Jewish perception is valuable to better understanding the passages we will review in John. One Jewish historian writes, "The rabbis were ideologically inclined toward the exclusion of women from Jewish religious life."[22] Webb gives a common benediction that was recited by Jewish males in their morning prayer: "Blessed be He who did not make me a Gentile; blessed be He who did not make me a boor [i.e., an ignorant peasant or slave]; blessed be He who did not make me a woman."[23]

Keener explains that "Jewish women attended synagogue and learned the law, but with possibly rare exceptions, were not raised to recite it the way most boys were."[24] Judaism was also influenced by the broader cultural view of women being inferior to men.

One source points out that women, like slaves and children, could not make moral decisions. This is reflected in the Talmud by the repeated references to women as manipulative seducers: "Do not converse much with women as this will ultimately lead you to unchastity."[25]

[18] Ruth Tucker, "The Changing Roles of Women in Ministry: The Early Church Through the 18th Century," in Discovering Biblical Equality: Complementarity Without Hierarchy, eds. Ronald W. Pierce and Rebecca Merrill Groothuis (Downers Grove: IVP, 2005), 26.

[19] Humphrey Mwangi Waweru, "Jesus and Ordinary Women in the Gospel of John: An African Perspective," Swedish Missiological Themes 96, no. 2 (2008), 142.

[20] Cohick, "Women, Children, and Families," 182.

[21] Evans, Woman in the Bible, 40.

[22] Steven Katz, ed., The Cambridge History of Judaism 4 (Cambridge: Cambridge University Press, 2006), 10.

[23] William Webb, Slaves, Women and Homosexuals: Exploring the Hermeneutics of Cultural Analysis (Downers Grove: IVP, 2001), 160.

[24] Craig S. Keener, preface to Paul, Women, and Wives, Marriage and Women's Ministry in the Letters of Paul, 8th ed. (Peabody: Hendrickson Publishers, 1992).

[25] Evans, Woman in the Bible, 35.

It is important to note that such restrictions on women are not biblically founded. For example, the requirement for a lower court for women cannot be found anywhere in the Old Testament. Leviticus 12:6 and 15:29 indicate that women were even expected to have an independent role in the sacrificial system. There is no sign in 1 Samuel 1 that there was any problem with Hannah approaching the sanctuary.

I do not intend to exhaust the historical context of the time of Jesus, but I hope these examples reinforce some of the earlier discussion in the opening chapters. As readers, we need contextual reference to understand the biblical message properly.

One last example on this point recalls a visit I made to Kenya. I was in a small Kenyan village with a group of pastors and their spouses. I was enjoying light conversation with one pastor when he pointed out his wife to me. "There she is—the fat one!" My Kenyan translator, more familiar with Canadian culture, immediately understood my alarm in hearing a man describe his wife as fat. He quickly leaned toward my ear and explained that in their village, being fat was a good thing because it meant that she had a good husband who provided for her. The insight of my translator gave me understanding of the pastor's reference to his wife being fat. His helpful explanation combatted my offence as it put things into perspective for me.

As we continue this discussion in light of Jesus' time and his interaction with women, we need to be careful not to impose *our* worldview on the text but rather to view the text in light of what we know of this ancient culture.

God's worldview transcends ours. That's the story we want to tap into.

CHAPTER 6
MARY MODELS DISCIPLESHIP 101 (JOHN 2:1–11)

FROM MARY, WE LEARN ABOUT DISCIPLESHIP. MARY'S RELATIONSHIP WITH JESUS was what prompted her actions. She had watched Jesus, learned from Jesus, grown in Jesus. We can be pretty brave and bold when we really grasp the possibilities of our faith! Mary's advantage was a fully immersed daily relationship with Jesus. What Mary did impacts the world 2,000 years later! Too often we limit our perspective to what we understand and can see, without the benefit of God's view.

During a school break one year, I took my two girls to see *The Bee Movie*. At the beginning of the movie a familiar television voice spoke over the text saying, "According to all known laws of aviation, there is no way a bee should be able to fly. The bees' wings are far too short to support their fat little bodies. Bees, of course, fly anyway, because bees don't care what humans think is possible."

This was unquestionably the most profound statement of the movie. The news flash might be reiterated another way—God and his creation do not need to follow *our* rules.

A comparable message was reported in *The Toronto Star* and other news media when 21-year-old Zack Dunlap was declared dead after being involved in a crash.[26] The results of the brain scan revealed no brain activity or blood flow at all. His family had even approved having his organs harvested, and they were paying their last respects when a pocket knife scratched the bottom of his foot and caused a reaction! The report added that Zack didn't remember much of the accident or what

---

[26] "'Dead' Man Revived Four Months Later," *The Toronto Star*, March 24, 2008, accessed January 30, 2017, https://www.thestar.com/news/world/2008/03/24/dead_man_revived_four_months_later.html.

happened afterwards; however, he did remember hearing the doctor declaring him dead. After being released 48 days later, the man said that he was feeling "pretty good."

What remains fascinating is that by all human ability to assess him, he was dead— and maybe he was! So it raises the question, could it be possible that some of the things in which we put stake as humans are beyond us or our own abilities and assessments? Mary, the mother of Jesus, thought so. As we see in the following story, Mary never lost sight of what might be possible when Jesus is with you. She was not the only one aware of the circumstances being faced at this wedding, but she was the only one to react the way she did. She was the only one who made the decision to entrust the challenge to Jesus. Here is her story:

The next day there was a wedding celebration in the village of Cana in Galilee. Jesus' mother was there, and Jesus and his disciples were also invited to the celebration. The wine supply ran out during the festivities, so Jesus' mother told him, "They have no more wine."

"Dear woman, that's not our problem," Jesus replied. "My time has not yet come."

But his mother told the servants, "Do whatever he tells you."

Standing nearby were six stone water jars, used for Jewish ceremonial washing. Each could hold twenty to thirty gallons. Jesus told the servants, "Fill the jars with water." When the jars had been filled, he said, "Now dip some out, and take it to the master of ceremonies." So the servants followed his instructions.

When the master of ceremonies tasted the water that was now wine, not knowing where it had come from (though, of course, the servants knew), he called the bridegroom over. "A host always serves the best wine first," he said. "Then, when everyone has had a lot to drink, he brings out the less expensive wine. But you have kept the best until now!"

This miraculous sign at Cana in Galilee was the first time Jesus revealed his glory. And his disciples believed in him. (John 2:1–11)

Mary put stake in the son whose actions she had pondered in her heart (Luke 2:19).

She put stake in what was beyond herself and her own assessment. Mary put stake in Jesus. For Mary, a social community event seemed fitting to make her request.

Mary understood the dilemma faced by the wedding hosts. She understood the social ramifications of running out of wine and was moved to action. In fact, "Mary did not underestimate herself because of gender bias. Her action influenced Jesus to supply the need and the servants to obey Jesus."[27]

As was the case then and is usually the case in even much of our contemporary culture, weddings are celebrations with family and friends being treated as special. We can't necessarily relate to the social pressure or expectations in this story, but we can relate to the excitement—the fun of being with friends and family celebrating a couple's love for each other. Wedding couples find pleasure in their guests' enjoyment of their day.

Personally, I enjoy giving wedding couples that pleasure. I especially enjoy giving that pleasure to my Italian friends and family! Perhaps you have participated in the seven- to eight-course meal that is usually offered at such weddings. After the several hours of eating, you demonstrate your version of the bunny hop, flex with exaggeration to "YMCA," and top it all off with a round of "Macarena." Thankfully, after all that exercise you are usually offered pizza and pastries before the drive home!

Mary, the disciples, and Jesus were privy to that kind of party within a different context. Running out of wine within her social framework was probably comparable to running out of food at some Italian weddings. Mary felt compassion for her hosts, an emotion that drove her to resolve the problem. She didn't know the answer herself, but she knew enough about Jesus to know that she could bring their concerns to him. Once she did, she could trust him with the outcome. She acted on what she knew.

One day my five-year-old was lying in bed with me, chatting about her life so far, when she reflected on her pre-birth and birth. Among her many questions and comments was one about being in my *stomach*. "I remember when I was in your stomach," she said. "I believe that I had to reach up and take food as it went by me, and that's how I ate." Well, it made sense. Babies are in mommies' tummies, and food passes through mommies' tummies. By her assessment, a little baby in a mommy's tummy must have to fend for herself!

What my daughter understood was based on the information she had. The stages of a baby's development, protective embryo, breakdown of nutrition, and isolation from mom's digestive track were not part of her equation, and therefore her full understanding was hindered. There is a risk in drawing firm conclusions on limited information. As a mom, I was impressed by her imagination, but what my five-year-old concluded was somewhat faulty.

Mary had a much greater pool of experience and certainty in her actions. She had known Jesus his whole lifetime on earth. She was confident that if she believed in

---

[27] Jey J. Kanagaraj, "The Profiles of Women in John: House-Bound or Christ-Bound?," *Evangelical Review Theology* 27, no. 1 (2003): 29.

Jesus and urged others to do the same, he *could* accomplish infinitely more than they might ask or think (Eph. 3:20). Her step of faith in her son would bring results beyond human assessment and ability.

Mary simply states the problem in verse 3: "They have no more wine." Jesus replies, calling his mom "woman," a fully acceptable form of address at the time.

His questioning why this should be her concern is intriguing. Jesus is drawn into her compassion for those hosting them, and he honours her faith. What is notable and encouraging to us is that by her faith came Jesus' first recorded miracle, one that happened even after Jesus first responded with "My time has not yet come."

The interaction exemplifies what Jesus says in Matthew 7:7: "Keep on asking, and you will receive what you ask for. Keep on seeking, and you will find. Keep on knocking, and the door will be opened to you." It certainly makes us wonder about prayer. Would the same events have happened had Mary not asked? It demonstrates for us how the "asking" and Jesus' response are somehow woven together to demonstrate our partnership in what he is actively doing. It also demonstrates how Mary's faith allowed God's intervention with Mary not fully knowing where that step would lead.

What is further noteworthy for us is that the actions of Jesus provide layers of depth—even foreshadowing his destiny and the symbolism of his death.

As we read the Gospels, we quickly discover that Jesus represents *himself* as the new wine. It is recorded in the Gospels of Mark and Matthew that he speaks of his blood, represented by wine, as being the mediating reality between God and people.

At the Last Supper, and as we remember each time we are given the opportunity for communion, Jesus said to his disciples when taking a cup of wine, "Drink from it, all of you; for this is my blood of the new covenant, which is poured out for many for the forgiveness of sins" (Matt. 26:27–28 NRSV).

Imagine the questions asked by the disciples in this moment! What could Jesus mean by referring to his blood as a new deal? Why would Jesus want his disciples to think of their needed forgiveness from sin while drinking wine?

N. T. Wright asks us, "What's your reaction to this extra-ordinary performance?"[28] He then adds that 1,000 years of Jewish celebrations are drawn into one event. So we can ask ourselves, as we participate in communion or the Eucharist, are we giving ourselves full opportunity to "go back in heart and mind to the original setting," to the wonder and the mystery and even the discomfort of this moment?[29]

Somehow, we can be immersed in its mystery. Followers of Jesus are invited to partake in the wine and bread, as they represent the forgiveness of sin and the gift of a new way of life. Wright explains, "Sin, a far greater slave master than Egypt had

---

[28] Tom Wright, *Matthew for Everyone* 2 (Westminster: John Knox Press, 2004), 156.

[29] Wright, *Matthew for Everyone* 2, 156.

ever been, would be defeated in the way that God defeated not only Egypt but the Red Sea."[30] Creating wine for his first miracle was not by accident.

When Mary called on Jesus at this wedding, whether she understood the full gamut of her actions or not, she gave her friends and family a preview of things to come. Mary's request ended up working in perfect harmony with God's plan for a new covenant—a new hope for the whole world!

Not coincidently, Jesus takes the water jars normally used for purification rites— the vessels used for cleansing and giving freedom from dirt or filth—and transforms the cleansing water into new wine, just as Jesus is the new wine that brings freedom from the dirt and filth we carry in our lives, called sin. It may be of interest that Jesus' first miracle involves water.

Sherri Brown develops her case for the imagery of water from Jewish tradition through to the life of Jesus. As we'll later see in the story of the Samaritan woman,

The water imagery in the Gospel of John reveals the power and presence of God uniquely embodied in Jesus as the Christ and Son of God, from incarnation to crucifixion and beyond into the lives of disciples across the ages.[31]

We have to wonder whether Mary was thinking back to her Jewish traditions of how water represented deliverance when God parted the waters for his chosen people and how the prophets and psalmists carried that theme of praise in prose. Or how our spiritual quest is satisfied: "My soul thirsts for God, for the living God" (Ps. 42:2 NRSV; see also Ps. 63:1, 143:6).

It's impossible to know how much Mary was piecing together from her traditions. Mary's attentiveness to Jesus, her quiet reflection through observation, and her memories of shepherds being led by angels to Jesus as a newborn, of Simeon declaring him the Saviour at 10 days old, and of wise men coming with gifts and worshipping him as a baby (Luke 2:8–15; Luke 2:25–28; Matt. 2:9) must have all been stored in her heart in preparation for this moment. Because what we store up in our hearts is what drives our actions (Luke 6:45). Mary models for us a very basic Christian discipline and practice.

While Mary is still required to perform the rearing functions of a mother responsible for her children's welfare, she yields to Jesus. She affirms her confidence in him by her statement "Do whatever he tells you."

As we are called to be leaders, we remain followers of the greatest leader of all time. So it was with Mary.

---

[30] Wright, *Matthew for Everyone* 2, 157. The story of the Israelites being freed from slavery is recorded in Exodus.

[31] Sherri Brown, "Water Imagery and the Power and Presence of God in the Gospel of John," *Theology Today* 72, no. 3 (2015): 289–98.

Jesus showed compassion to Mary's role as his mother even at the end as she stood by the cross. "When Jesus saw his mother standing there beside the disciple he loved, he said to her, 'Dear woman, here is your son.' And he said to this disciple, 'Here is your mother.' And from then on this disciple took her into his home" (John 19:26–28). Kanagaraj sees this scene as highly significant in establishing the emerging "Christian community (represented by one male—the beloved disciple; and one female—Mary) that will derive its life from the cross."[32] He concludes that this final act before saying "it is finished" on the cross envisions a "community of new disciples in which men and women have equal roles to play."

Mary's ongoing ponderings culminated at the cross. She accepted her changing role and the tremendous challenges of her emerging calling. Mary accepted the fate of her son, remaining with Jesus even while she grieved his physical pain, torture, ridicule, and abandonment. She endured with him beside the cross.

Even following the death of Jesus, Mary gathered with the disciples, praying and participating in his call and mission. Mary served her call in faith by her giftedness. She experienced a deeply rooted and growing relationship with Jesus.

Just as he does with us, Jesus showed an interest in Mary's life—in the things that mattered to her. We are limited in what we know about how Mary adapted to life changes, but we do know that as she remained with Jesus, Jesus remained with her (John 15). That's a promise and an encouragement we gain from Mary's life!

Mary's source for perseverance—Jesus—offers comfort to women feeling pressed by the many activities of life. This can certainly happen throughout the journey of different life seasons.

Writer and speaker John Ortberg talks about a young mom of toddlers who confessed that her life of prayer and Bible reading was much more regimented prior to parenthood. Ortberg explains that caring for two young children, offering daily expressions of gratitude and prayers for help and patient acceptance of trials, can become a kind of school for transformation.

No question, many moms would agree that the constant exercising of putting others before yourself is a developed discipline that helps define character. When we bring God's Spirit in conversation with those daily challenges, we develop endurance. Paul explains in Romans that endurance comes from facing trials, which develops strength of character and ultimately hope (Rom. 5).

So our season of life is no barrier to having Christ formed in us or allowing our story to merge with his. In fact, it is often in walking through the valleys that we grow. Every moment is a chance to learn from Jesus how to live in the kingdom of God. Paul writes in his letter to the Colossians, "Whatever you do, in word or deed, do everything in...Jesus" (Col. 3:17 NRSV).

---

[32] Kanagaraj, "The Profiles of Women in John," 31.

Mary demonstrates for us what discipleship can look like. In doing so, she shows us how discipleship enters into God's story.

CHAPTER 7

A FEMALE APOSTLE IS THE FIRST EVANGELIST

(JOHN 4:3–30)

AT TIMES, WE CAN FEEL IMMOBILE, STAGNANT, UNINSPIRED. OUR GIFT FROM JESUS is to be mobilized to new opportunities, new insight, a new race, a new culture, a new hope, new possibilities. Becoming the story of Jesus means that we participate in what Jesus is doing. As we grow in Jesus, we become aware of the many ways he is moving all around us.

The Samaritan woman reminds us that God calls us beyond the expectations of others—or ourselves. Her example guides us along a path of adventure and possibility. We see in the Samaritan woman a road of discovery at the invitation of Jesus as well as the opportunity to inspire in others that same invitation. She is an apostle and evangelist. We see in her one becoming part of God's story—in multiple ways. That's the story we want to emulate!

Here is the story of the Samaritan woman:

[Jesus] left Judea and returned to Galilee.

He had to go through Samaria on the way. Eventually he came to the Samaritan village of Sychar, near the field that Jacob gave to his son Joseph. Jacob's well was there; and Jesus, tired from the long walk, sat wearily beside the well about noontime. Soon a Samaritan woman came to draw water, and Jesus said to her, "Please give me a drink." He was alone at the time because his disciples had gone into the village to buy some food.

The woman was surprised, for Jews refuse to have anything to do with Samaritans. She said to Jesus, "You are a Jew, and I am a Samaritan woman. Why are you asking me for a drink?"

Jesus replied, "If you only knew the gift God has for you and who you are speaking to, you would ask me, and I would give you living water."

"But sir, you don't have a rope or a bucket," she said, "and this well is very deep. Where would you get this living water? And besides, do you think you're greater than our ancestor Jacob, who gave us this well? How can you offer better water than he and his sons and his animals enjoyed?"

Jesus replied, "Anyone who drinks this water will soon become thirsty again. But those who drink the water I give will never be thirsty again. It becomes a fresh, bubbling spring within them, giving them eternal life."

"Please, sir," the woman said, "give me this water! Then I'll never be thirsty again, and I won't have to come here to get water."

"Go and get your husband," Jesus told her.

"I don't have a husband," the woman replied.

Jesus said, "You're right! You don't have a husband— for you have had five husbands, and you aren't even married to the man you're living with now. You certainly spoke the truth!"

"Sir," the woman said, "you must be a prophet. So tell me, why is it that you Jews insist that Jerusalem is the only place of worship, while we Samaritans claim it is here at Mount Gerizim, where our ancestors worshiped?"

Jesus replied, "Believe me, dear woman, the time is coming when it will no longer matter whether you worship the Father on this mountain or in Jerusalem. You Samaritans know very little about the one you worship, while we Jews know all about him, for salvation comes through the Jews. But the time is coming— indeed it's here now—when true worshipers will worship the Father in spirit and in truth. The Father is looking for those who will worship him that way. For God is Spirit, so those who worship him must worship in spirit and in truth."

The woman said, "I know the Messiah is coming—the one who is called Christ. When he comes, he will explain everything to us."

Then Jesus told her, "I am the Messiah!"

Just then his disciples came back. They were shocked to find him talking to a woman, but none of them had the nerve to ask, "What do you want with her?" or "Why are you talking to her?" The woman left her water jar beside the well and ran back to the village, telling everyone, "Come and see a man who told me everything I ever did! Could he possibly be the Messiah?" So the people came streaming from the village to see him. (John 4:3–30)

A number of years ago the expression "TMI" (too much information) was commonly used when people revealed more personal information than their audience wanted to hear. Most of us have been in situations where too much has been said. Imagine the scenario: You are sitting in a public place across from someone who is speaking loudly. As the person's voice elevates, you become increasingly aware of the people around you beginning to eavesdrop on your conversation. You start to squirm in your seat and simultaneously daydream about the many other places you would rather be.

The truth is that we usually reveal information to people only as our comfort level with them increases. But the interesting thing about Jesus, in the passage just quoted, is that he leaps right into the Samaritan woman's personal history, causing her to reveal more than she normally would have—and he does it very comfortably in casual conversation with her. It's almost as though Jesus is masterfully cutting to the heart of the matter to maximize his time with her. When Jesus tells the woman to get her husband, she answers honestly, and Jesus praises her. Jo-Ann Brant calls her response a "painful admission," and this is what moves the conversation from playful banter to sincere conversation.[33]

Alan Loy McGinnis, author of *The Friendship Factor*, says something that we need to hear: "If we acknowledge our dark side we will become whole. In ways we don't fully understand, self-disclosure helps us to see things, feel things, imagine things, and hope for things that we could never have thought possible."[34] Brant's observation also makes this point when she talks about the Samaritan woman's mission. What the woman ends up revealing about Jesus to others is what he knew about her.[35]

This is what we see at the close of the recorded conversation in John. We are told that the Samaritan woman went back to the city saying, "Come and see a man who told me everything I ever did!" (John 4:29). She was aware of her excessive disclosure to someone she had just met and his apparent comfort with that information. Perhaps the exchange had perpetuated self-awareness of her dark side... perhaps she felt new things about herself through the disclosure. No doubt she was feeling, imagining, and hoping for things that she had probably never previously entertained.

This Samaritan woman encountered Jesus. And in this encounter, she meets a listening ear who accepted her. In the book *How to Make Friends and Influence People*, an oldie but goodie, Dale Carnegie says, "Instead of condemning people, let's try to understand them. Let's try to figure out why they do what they do. That's a lot more profitable and intriguing than criticism; and it breeds sympathy, tolerance and kindness."[36]

---

[33] Jo-Ann A. Brant, *John*, Paideia Commentaries on the New Testament (Grand Rapids: Baker Academic, 2011), 85.

[34] Alan Loy McGinnis, *The Friendship Factor* (Minneapolis: Augsburg Books, 1979), 30.

[35] Brant, *John*, 86.

[36] Dale Carnegie, *How to Win Friends and Influence People* (New York: First Pocket Books, 1998), 46.

How we see people affects whether we listen to them, whether we are interested in them, what we entrust to them, and how we introduce them.

Jesus accepted who this woman was and listened to her questions attentively.

When one of my daughters was just a little under three, I called her from the kitchen. She, I thought, was in the living room taking her time and not listening. I was hurriedly trying to get us packed up to go to a children's outdoor park and zoo. Every time I called her I heard her say something, but I couldn't make out what it was. Finally, I said, "Okay, if you are not over here by the time I count to three, we are not going to the zoo." I started counting, one... two..., and I was just about to say three when my little girl came running into the kitchen with her pants down and a piece of toilet paper hanging from her backside. My heart sank.

Any slight aspiration I might have had for winning the Mother of the Year Award immediately vanished! I was distracted. I couldn't hear what she was trying to tell me. I made wrong assumptions. I wasn't listening. All she wanted from me at that moment was for me to hear her.

We all want to be heard. We want to be understood. We like being asked questions about ourselves. Granted, if you are a mother of teenagers you might be disagreeing with this claim, since you may be told that you ask too many questions. Melissa Trevathan and Sissy Goff in their book *All You Need to Know About Raising Girls*[37] deal with the reality of the narcissistic years and how teenage girls, in particular, seek to emulate *older* girls and women—anyone except their mother. The authors address how almost overnight it seems that a mother's relationship with her daughters changes; suddenly their peers take on a brand new significance. Often teenage girls seek that understanding and sense of being known among their peers. Take comfort as a parent, for the writers also claim that, while it may not be as evident, a parent's ear is still important.

For the rest of us, someone who knows how to really listen is a rare gift to find. Jesus listens. Jesus knows that we want to be heard, understood, and listened to more than we want advice. Jesus really listens.

When the disciples return and see Jesus with the Samaritan woman, they are justifiably shocked (v. 27). Their reaction is only weakly translated from the Greek by the word "marvelled" or "astonished."[38] Theologian Duncan Derrett notes that "Samaritan women were suspected of immorality generally and a rabbinical maxim tells us that all Samaritan women were to be deemed perpetual menstruants—an unpleasant idea which suggests sterility."[39] The Mishnah, which is the oral tradition of the Jewish law, is also telling in that it may very well "reflect the views of Jesus'

---

[37] Melissa Trevathan and Sissy Goff, *All You Need to Know About Raising Girls* (Grand Rapids: Zondervan, 2007).

[38] Alton Wedel, "John 4:5–26 (5–42)," *Interpretation* 31 (1977): 407.

[39] J. Duncan Derrett, "The Samaritan Woman's Purity (John 4:4–52)," *Evangelical Quarterly* 60, no. 4 (1988): 291–298.

contemporaries: 'Rabbi Eliezer used to say, "He that eats of the bread of Samaritans is as one who eats the flesh of swine"' (m. Seb. 8:10)."[40]

The actions of Jesus defied public decency and rules of purity. Brant explains that even the fact that Jesus is sitting is significant, as his head is below the woman's.[41] Oblivious to public opinion and disregarding expected rules of conduct, Jesus enters into a theological conversation that is supposed to surpass the mental capacity of women (vs 9–26). Brant explains that the grammatical syntax "emphasizes the rapid pace of the dialogue."[42] J. Ramsay Michaels says that she proves herself as a worthy debating partner.[43]

Jesus, the liberator, transcended social rules and norms. The disciples knew enough not to say anything. No one said, "What do you want?" or "Why are you speaking with her?"

By Jesus' actions, there is increased understanding and recognition on the woman's part, evidenced by her responses to him. The Samaritan woman's understanding of Jesus' self-revelation is progressive. Alton Wedel tells us, "She is progressively released from that which is below to that which is from above, from earthy concerns to eternal concerns, from bondage to freedom, from legalism and guilt to true worship."[44]

Because of his shocking social actions, the Samaritan woman becomes a follower of Jesus. Her one encounter with Jesus changes her role, changes her perspective, and changes her life. Her new role becomes one with a calling—with a mission. Just as the disciples are called to "come follow" (Matt. 4:19; Mark 1:17) so too the Samaritan woman leaves her pot behind and heads for her new beginning.

Sent by Christ, she confesses the Messiah to others, the message that she is instructed to relay by the instructions of Jesus himself. And we know that people are drawn to Jesus through her efforts (John 4:39).

Many Samaritans from the village believed in Jesus because the woman had said, "He told me everything I ever did!" When they came out to see him, they begged him to stay in their village. So he stayed for two days, long enough for many more to hear his message and believe. Then they said to the woman, "Now we believe, not just because of what you told us, but because we have heard him ourselves. Now we know that he is indeed the Savior of the world." (John 4:39–42)

---

[40] Brant, *John*, 83.

[41] Brant, *John*, 84.

[42] Brant, *John*.

[43] J. Ramsey Michaels, *The Gospel of John* (Grand Rapids: William B. Eerdmans Publishing, 2010).

[44] Wedel, "John 4:5–26 (5–42)," 410.

The Samaritan woman is a woman with a story to tell. In fact, she is the first person to hear from the lips of the Saviour "I am he" (John 4:26 NRSV).[45] Jesus, who refused the title of Messiah from the Jews, accepted it from this Samaritan.

Donald Bloesch comments, "He [Jesus] chose to reveal the mystery of the gospel, as well as his Messianic identity, to an unknown Samaritan woman (John 4). As 'the enlightened one,' she was sent out to become the first evangelist to the Samaritans."[46]

The Samaritan woman's call was that of being commissioned with fresh news to be delivered for her day. With 2,000 years of Christian experience behind us, we may find the call of Jesus different—or is it?

Similar to the Samaritan woman, today we are commissioned with a task to hear the words of Jesus through the fresh eyes of our generation. What that looks like within the gift set that God has given to each person remains the task of whoever has been commissioned.

No one else in history is like you. No one else has been created just like you. No one in history is uniquely gifted and placed in your unique environment, with your unique experience and background, with abilities unique to you. No full combination of your attributes has ever existed before—ever. You are fearfully and wonderfully made (Psalm 139) for this time in history to partner with the living God, the Creator of the universe! So in a sense, you are the first and only one divinely called to your unique purpose.

Much has been written on possible new forms of church and our call to be missional. Most Christian leaders are well aware that the face of church is changing. Their consensus is that how we have been "doing" church isn't necessarily leading people to Jesus. Those of us who have met Jesus long to see him introduced to others and seek to help people plow through the stereotyping of recent Christian history, which sometimes blocks that introduction.

Some leaders talk about the resurgence of spiritual disciplines to bring people to a deeper experience with Jesus. Models of church practiced in the last three decades, in many cases, assumed more of a performance-based worship. Newer modes of doing church since then have been challenging people to more direct involvement.

At one point, we assumed people would come through our doors and want to stay; now we are realizing the challenge of bringing Jesus into the community. Many pastors are feeling an inner awakening to become more like Jesus—to live more like Jesus in their own community.

Our challenge to convey the good news of Jesus is just as real in our current generation as it was with the Samaritan woman. Our commission is comparable to

---

[45] Q. M. Adams, *Neither Male nor Female: A Study of the Scriptures* (Devon: Arthur H. Stockwell Ltd., 1973), 91.

[46] Donald G. Bloesch, *Is the Bible Sexist?* (Westchester: Crossway Books, 1982), 43.

the call of Jesus 2,000 years ago. A true encounter with Jesus can't be contained or stifled—it needs to be shared. We, like the Samaritan woman, are commissioned by Jesus to reveal him to a new generation. We as the commissioned ones just may be the first glimpse people have of a real encounter with Jesus. We are entitled to hold out the gift of God's love in Jesus—so often misunderstood and wrongly presented.

When my daughters were younger, they would get pretty excited when they had a gift or surprise for someone. It would take everything for them not to reveal what it was. With a wide grin and a gleam in their eyes, they would say something like, "Mom, I can't tell you, but we got you something pretty special."

The exchange would usually continue with me saying, "Don't tell me; I like surprises!" You see, unlike my brother, who would sneak down, unwrap, and rewrap all his gifts before Christmas because he couldn't bear the anticipation, I'm one of those people who enjoy the savouring of possibilities. I like the anticipation. So the holder of the information has to keep the secret.

But when we carry exciting news, it *calls* us to share it! Generally, we can't wait to see the receivers' reaction. We want to experience with them the joy they will know in that moment when the news is delivered. We want to be part of creating a memory. We want to imagine with them how this news will impact their lives and what significance it will bring them.

That was the case one time at 2 o'clock in the morning when I first looked at the clock following a brief sleep. After a full day of meetings and picking up a pregnancy test, I retired early to my bed in the simple surroundings of a monastery. Pastors' meetings usually mean accommodations that fit modest budgets. My husband and I had been married six months, and with each month that passed, I was feeling a rising anxiety, wondering whether we would soon know the blessing of a baby in our lives. Anyone who has experienced infertility knows that six months of waiting is really nothing; however, as parents-to-be who were more on the mature side and who had journeyed with many friends handling the stress of not being able to conceive, we knew apprehension.

Ideally, the test is most accurate in the morning. So after waiting it out and staring at the clock every half hour until 5 a.m., I decided that I was ready! In much less than the stated 30 seconds, two strong red lines appeared in the window of the tester. It was positive! I—we—were going to have a baby! A whole other day remained before me of not being able to share my good news with my husband. In hindsight, it was probably one of the longest days of my life!

How could I do justice as a messenger to the news that I held? Several moments of daydreaming throughout the day helped me entertain a variety of delivery methods for my news before I settled on a greeting card, strategically placed. There it was, in a sealed envelope on my husband's computer keyboard, waiting for him to arrive home. I excitedly waited, listening to his steps leading into his office. He read the following:

Though I'm really tiny yet,
Already the master's hand I've met.
I'm an answer to my parents' prayer,
My mom and dad who have God's fav'r
And in the next 9 months I'll grow;
September I'll arrive in tow.
You get to be my guide in life;
Modelling God's plan as man and wife.
Keep very close to God, I ask;
'cause teaching him to me will be your task
I can't wait to meet you late this year,
I hear my new extended clan will cheer.
Dad, please pray for me…
And one day soon, your face I'll see!
Much love, "little" Wolfe

As my husband very quickly assessed, I was the holder of great news. Prior to this moment of disclosure, I was the only one on earth who carried this wonderful truth; I got to convey the news to others!

Now imagine being that Samaritan woman, the very first to be told the real story about Jesus (outside of the heavenly pronouncements before and at his birth).[47] Imagine! Imagine being entrusted with the world's best news ever!

Jesus gave that first-time honour to an unknown Samaritan woman! Michaels says, "Six chapters later, the 'Jews' in Jerusalem by contrast are still trying to determine whether Jesus is making this claim and yet here he does it with the Samaritan woman on her soil."[48]

And this seems to be no accident! Michaels claims "that there is a precision to the location" and even to the sixth hour (noon), which coincidently is the same hour as Jesus' later crucifixion.[49]

Michaels ponders the story of Nicodemus visiting Jesus (John 3), compared to this visit with the Samaritan woman. The Samaritan woman meets Jesus at noon with no foreknowledge of whom she is meeting. Interestingly, Nicodemus goes to meet Jesus after dark, knowing that Jesus is sent by God (John 3:2). "Knowing

[47] Adams, *Neither Male nor Female*, 91.
[48] Michaels, *The Gospel of John*, 255.
[49] Michaels, *The Gospel of John*, 236.

nothing of Jesus she (the Samaritan Woman) simply comes to the spring at high noon for water—unlike Nicodemus who came at night professing allegiance."[50]

Nicodemus is told that the Son comes into the world to save the world. The Samaritan is explicitly told by Jesus that he is the Messiah (v. 26). She then tells her story so that others have their interest piqued to hear more and then *know* that Jesus is the Saviour of the world (John 4:42).

God's design seemed to be very much in this encounter. This meeting takes place at the well of Jacob. We first hear about this spot in Genesis 48:22. The water came from an underground spring. Jesus starts talking about *living* water, and the metaphor fits. The water Jesus describes as coming from him is a "fresh, bubbling spring within them," meaning "abundance, a continuing, self-replenishing supply of good fresh water that never runs dry."[51]

The Samaritan woman may be mocking Jesus when she asks whether Jesus is greater than "our ancestor Jacob" just before Jesus makes the claim of living water. Either way, there certainly seems to be a bridging with the Jews in her referring to their common ancestry. Keener implies, "Samaritans deceptively tried to profess themselves Jews when matters are going well for the Jewish community, but admit the truth by denying their kinship when hard times come to the Jewish people (*Josephus Ant.* 9.291; 11.340–341)."[52]

But this too seems part of God's plan. One commentary from an intercultural perspective says this: "The discontinuity between Jew and Samaritan was appropriated politically and racially in their own contexts. In some of the readings, the well of Jacob is then interpreted as a symbolic point of reconciliation."[53]

It is in fact at this pivotal point of reconciliation that we see ourselves. The location of worship as designated by the Samaritans and the Jews is no longer important. Instead, worship is described as true and explained as new. As readers of the Gospel of John, we can see ourselves "no longer as Jews or Gentiles, but as Christians, a 'new race' or 'third race' who worship in a new way. This will mean worshipping God as the Father through Jesus the Son."[54] Here at Jacob's well, the perceptive eye gets a full view of God's plan to save the world. No longer is there Jew or Gentile, slave or free, male and female. For you *(we)* are all one in Christ Jesus. Together, we are united as the bride of Christ for which Jesus has come!

McHugh refers to John the Baptist having prepared the way for Jesus and the imagery of the Bridegroom coming for his bride:

---

[50] Michaels, *The Gospel of John*, 238.

[51] Michaels, *The Gospel of John*, 244.

[52] Craig Keener, *The Gospel of John: A Commentary* 1 (Peabody: Hendrickson Publishers, 2003), 602.

[53] Hans de Wit et al., eds., *Through the Eyes of Another: Intercultural Reading of the Bible* (Amsterdam: Institute of Mennonite Studies, 2004), 323.

[54] Michaels, *The Gospel of John*, 255.

John, in describing Jesus as arriving exhausted at Jacob's Well, is presenting the bridegroom coming in person to Samaria, to take home his long-lost bride (compare Hos 2.14–23; 14:4–7). The scene depicts the fulfilment of the final words uttered by the Baptist, that the bridegroom of Israel is come (Jn 3:28–30). The bridegroom is prepared to travel any distance to bring the errant home.[55]

The Samaritan woman gets it! Her response was prompt and full of zeal. Jesus knew her. He knew how she would respond. Not only was she part of a much bigger plan that was still to unfold, he tapped into her passions and called her to something God had already designed for her to do. She got to be the *first* to share God's good news with others.

It raises for us so many questions. What is God tapping into in terms of your gifts and passions? What is he revealing to you that can be offered as good news to the world around you? How will your encounter with Jesus make a difference?

The Samaritan woman had the privilege of being the first!

I *get* that. I love being the first when it comes to calling people on their birthdays or conveying good news about other family members. My family knows that about me, but I dare say I'm not alone in that quest. I've observed in my girls the same enjoyment.

When my girls were smaller and spoke to Grandma on the speakerphone and I suggested in the background that they tell her we were going to the park, usually the older one would begin to tell her. In seconds, tension erupted as the younger one cried out, "No, I want to tell Grandma!" Of course, the volume of the girls' voices outdoing each other destroyed the message, but the zeal and enthusiasm in being the "one" to give the news became the pursuit of significance.

The Samaritan woman's call was unique to her, and she couldn't wait to tell others. She was a woman with a story to tell. She alone was the one at that instance in history to carry the truth about Jesus. She was the first!

Some early church fathers granted her the title "apostle," a term often reserved for the 12 followers but simply meaning "one sent." Incidentally, the word *apostle* is used prior to the time of Jesus in the Old Testament, and apostleship is listed among the spiritual gifts assigned by the Holy Spirit (Eph. 4; 1 Cor. 12). While the Christian church has historically concurred to reserve the word for those who were commissioned by Jesus to found the church, C. K. Barrett, in *The Signs of an Apostle*, writes that the sending by Jesus and proclamation of a message are the chief work of an apostle.[56]

[55] John F. McHugh, *A Critical and Exegetical Commentary on John 1–4*, International Critical Commentary, eds. G. I. Davies and G. N. Stanton (New York: T & T Clark, 2009), 272.

[56] C. K. Barrett, *The Signs of an Apostle* (London: Epworth Press, 1969), 13.

The apostle Paul was commissioned by Jesus after the original 12. In his writings, we see his understanding of apostleship as being a servant and a missionary. In Barrett's criteria for apostleship, the function of an apostle is supported by and made possible by the Holy Spirit.[57] The effectiveness of apostleship depends on two key points: the continued operation of the Holy Spirit and the existence of the apostolic testimony.

When Jesus calls us for a task he reinforces what he is doing through his Spirit. He never leaves us without support when it is something he has commissioned us to do. Since his resurrection, Jesus has left us with his Spirit in order that his work might be continued through us (John 16:3).

Following the Samaritan woman's testimony, people believed that Jesus was "the Savior of the world" (John 4:42) because they had also heard it for themselves—as she did—from Jesus himself. That's apostleship; that's evangelism!

The Samaritan woman gives us cause to consider what Jesus is speaking to all of us, what Jesus calls us to, and how we personally might participate in the greatest story ever told—and become more and more part of that story!

---

[57] Barrett's four criteria for apostleship are the following: God's divine choice for servants; appointed to behold God in history through Jesus; hear, keep and obey the word of Jesus; their function is supported and made possible by the Holy Spirit. The effectiveness of the four elements depends on two key points: the continued operation of the Holy Spirit and the existence of the apostolic testimony.

CHAPTER 8

MARTHA:

CONVICTING FAITH LEADS TO A DEMONSTRATION OF THE POWER OF GOD
(JOHN 11:17–27)

THERE'S A STORY OFTEN TOLD OF A TIGHTROPE WALKER ABOUT TO TREAD OVER Niagara Falls pushing a wheelbarrow. Below are the cheering crowds yelling "I believe you can do it!" along with lots of hooting and hollering. The tightrope walker looks down at the crowds and asks with genuine inquisitiveness, "You really believe I can do this?" "Yes," says the crowd, "we believe in you!" The tightrope walker looks again at the enthusiastic group of people below him and says, "Okay, if you really believe in me, would someone like to volunteer to get into the wheelbarrow?"

In the story about raising Lazarus, Martha takes the lead by showing us what it means to get into the wheelbarrow! Martha knows what she believes and acts upon it. We witness a surrender to what she knows as being true about Jesus, and here lies her hope. She towers over the others with a convicting faith that leads us into the power of God. Her recognition of who Jesus is and her movement of faith for his intervention allow Martha to witness God at work! Furthermore, her faith allows those around her an opportunity to also see God at work. We learn from Martha how to stand on what we know about the Saviour of the world, the Son of God, the one who has come into the world.

John tells us the story of Martha after her brother died:

When Jesus arrived at Bethany, he was told that Lazarus had already been in his grave for four days. Bethany was only a few miles down the road from Jerusalem, and many of the people had come to console Martha and Mary in their loss. When Martha got word that Jesus was coming, she went to meet him. But Mary stayed in the house. Martha said to Jesus, "Lord, if only you had been here, my brother would not have died. But even now I know that God will give you whatever you ask."

Jesus told her, "Your brother will rise again."

"Yes," Martha said, "he will rise when everyone else rises, at the last day."

Jesus told her, "I am the resurrection and the life. Anyone who believes in me will live, even after dying. Everyone who lives in me and believes in me will never ever die. Do you believe this, Martha?"

"Yes, Lord," she told him. "I have always believed you are the Messiah, the Son of God, the one who has come into the world from God." (John 11:17–27)

The more important characteristic of apostles, according to Barrett, is not that they understand all of the teachings of Jesus but that they act in obedience to his teachings as they are known.[58] Martha demonstrates faith in a Hebrews 11 sort of way: "Faith shows the reality of what we hope for; it is the evidence of things we cannot see" (Heb. 11:1).

It's Martha's zeal in greeting Jesus that speaks to us.

Martha hears that Jesus is on his way and goes to meet him (v. 20), while her sister waits at home. Here in the midst of many people comforting Mary and Martha for their loss, Martha just leaves.

No doubt, Jesus was pleased with Martha's eagerness to see his intervention. Perhaps Martha and Mary wondered why Jesus was delayed by an extra two days before responding to their message (John 11:6). On the other hand, his disciples were probably confused about why Jesus would want to return at all, since the Jews had just tried to stone him (John 11:8).

Martha asserts that her brother wouldn't have died had Jesus been there. There is evidence of a friendship factor that gives both Martha and Mary permission to be honest and comfortable with Jesus. Mary repeats the same refrain: "Lord, if only you had been here, my brother would not have died" (v. 21). Even though her brother has died, there is hope in her actions. There is a sense of surrender in her words to Jesus when she says, "But even now I know that God will give you whatever you ask" (v. 22).

Beyond what the disciples, or even Martha, see, perhaps the delay was deliberate. Was there maybe through this event a foreshadowing that death produces a plentiful harvest of new lives? (John 12:24 and Rom. 6:4.)

This was a moment in history unique to Martha's life and relationship with Jesus. But every day, God's people, men and women, are given opportunities to express their faith. Every day we can take the words of Jesus to heart as we face a variety of circumstances, be they challenging, difficult, joy filled, or painful. Jesus continues

[58] Barrett, The Signs of an Apostle, 67.

to whisper to our spirits, "Did I not tell you that if you believed, you would see the glory of God?"

Martha demonstrated a belief that Jesus creates pathways where none would otherwise exist. She believed that even the mere presence of Jesus would have made the difference in her brother not dying. And still that same presence held out hope to revert or redeem or transform or do something that made everything right.

Jesus replies, "Your brother will rise again" (v. 23). Martha's next words almost seem anticipatory, or clarifying, or confirming, or probing. Certainly they seem to be breathed with hope: "He will rise when everyone else rises" (v. 24).

So Jesus then turns the conversation away from her brother and to himself: "I am the resurrection and the life...Do you believe this, Martha?" (v. 25–26).

Suddenly, the conversation focuses on what Martha believes about Jesus. Her perception of Jesus, who he is, and what he can do all need to be addressed before anything more is said.

It all comes down to Martha's relationship with Jesus. What Martha believes about Jesus is poised to make a difference to others. Martha's connection to Jesus will produce a conduit that extends into the lives of others. What Jesus does next shows that!

We, as followers of Jesus, have that same opportunity in all our interactions, relationships, opportunities, and challenges. We too can be a conduit that extends into the lives of others.

I have a friend who announced that she was returning to Montreal after having lived in our neighbourhood for three years. While long-distance friendships are doable, her departure meant the end of a season. As I reflected on our friendship, I was haunted by the question "Did I impart anything into her life over those years that brought her closer to Jesus?" I felt I had failed. It was easy for me to recall missed opportunities and to wonder whether God's radiance in me paled in light of my own shortcomings.

In my discouragement, I picked up a book called *The Life You've Always Wanted*.[59] The title certainly gave the impression that it would instill hope. I began reading the first chapter. The writer, John Ortberg, begins by expressing some of his own disappointments in himself—his self-absorption in needing to look more chiselled and handsome than his colleagues at his high school reunion and, mostly, his nagging sense that all is not as it should be. He talks about watching his children sleep at night and about being the father he would like to be:

> I want to create moments of magic, I want them to remember laughing until the tears flow, I want to read to them and make the books come alive so they love

---

[59] John Ortberg, *The Life You've Always Wanted* (Grand Rapids: Zondervan Publishing, 1998).

to read, I want to have slow sweet talks with them as they are getting ready to close their eyes, have food fights, play tennis, chase fireflies and hold them and pray for them in a way that makes them feel cherished.[60]

Needless to say, his reflections were not helpful. I found myself relating to the limitations he saw in himself and how I too wanted those things for my children. I began to recall the times that I had watched my children sleep and had considered my day's activities. I remembered those moments when I lacked patience or had a quick temper.

"Tomorrow morning," I resolved, "will be a new day!" I would start the next morning asking for patience and would give special attention so not to miss significant moments. I would learn to savour those distractions to my personal agenda and begin to see them as God's creative direction.

I read further as Ortberg took inventory of his day and remembered the instance when he yelled at his daughter for spilling her milk—then saw in her face the tiny wound she would now have in her heart—and how he missed helping his kids resolve conflict when they were trapped in a disagreement that led to physical contact. "Yikes!" I blurted out. I questioned the number of times I had missed opportunities to meet some of those same challenges. I felt doomed and defeated. Like Ortberg, I was caught up in a whirlwind of lost opportunity and failure. This moment of truth failed to comfort me as was promised by the title. I knew there was only one place to turn. So I closed the book and decided to read instead *The Paper Bag Princess*!

No, I didn't. Instead, I read on. I read on because I am convinced that when I fail, there is still hope. When my day didn't include all of my grandiose plans to create a balance of play and educational experiences for my children or I lacked patience in telling my girls not to argue with each other, I believed that the next day was another opportunity for growth.

When I'm feeling grumpy and inadequate as a friend, a mother, a wife, or a person in general, I believe in hope. Because I believe that what Jesus sees is different. I believe that he sees *me* differently. And I believe *that* awareness of my disappointment in me is a first step to being better.

So I live in the hope of Christ's transforming grace. Paul writes to the Galatians, "I feel as if I'm going through labor pains for you again, and they will continue until Christ is fully developed in your lives" (Gal. 4:19). If I were to stay in my disappointment I would be shortchanging the life that God has called me to live—and shortchanging those around me. God desires that I live increasingly in deeper relationship with Jesus, in my unique place in the world and in my particular season of life.

---

[60] Ortberg, *The Life You've Always Wanted*, 14.

In these short few lines that we read of Martha, she couldn't get to Jesus fast enough to share her disappointment. Because of her friendship with Jesus she had a developed understanding of who he was and how hope was guaranteed because of him.

Martha took a moment to recognize her own limitations. She knew that looking through her eyes meant that her brother was dead. But she also knew that looking through the eyes of Jesus meant something different. Jesus sees differently than we do.

Martha put her hope in what she saw in Jesus. It was by doing so that she was faced with the resurrection being not just a doctrine—but a person.[61]

With each step that Martha takes toward Jesus in this exchange, Jesus meets her. Jesus responds that Lazarus will rise again, and Martha responds with what she knows.

What is interesting is that the concept of a resurrection from the dead is not something that is specifically stated in the Old Testament, prior to Jesus. The Sadducees didn't believe in a resurrection at all. In the book of Acts, we read about how the Sadducees were "greatly disturbed because [the apostles] were teaching the people and proclaiming in Jesus the resurrection from the dead" (Acts 4:2 NASB). The Pharisees believed in a resurrection that was probably comparable to resuscitation or the resurrection of the spirit or soul but not the resurrection of the body.

Martha probably shares in the Pharisaic view. She repeats what she understands of resurrection teaching to Jesus, and he responds. In that very moment, a great theological truth is revealed.

Where the Samaritan woman was the first to be enlightened as to the Messiah, Martha is the first to hear the words of Christ in his claim as the resurrection. Jesus chooses a woman to reveal to that he *is* the resurrection—an important factor in this moment in history. He had kept a tight circle of men around him with whom he had shared many thoughts, but Martha is the person to whom he first reveals his fate and mission as the resurrection.

Jesus connects with the understanding Martha has and uses that opportunity to give further insight.

This is a significant point. Often we miss hearing people's departure point of understanding and move beyond or before what they are prepared to hear. The only way Jesus can further enlighten Martha is to meet her thought patterns and the hope that is underlined in what she is articulating.

We can learn from how Jesus listened to others. Sometimes we suspect that people in conversation drift off and start thinking about their next point—not Jesus!

---

[61] N. T. Wright, *John for Everyone* 2 (Louisville: Westminster Knox Press, 2003), 7.

He didn't impatiently jump in before Martha was finished. He listened to what she had to say and then responded—profoundly.

We get that same opportunity with people every day—that is, practicing active listening. When my husband and I were first married, he would often claim that I would march into conversations without context and expect him to know what I was talking about. As our relationship has deepened through the years, I have noticed that, rather than be frustrated by this, he is now able to jump into that context without the benefit of my explanations. He watches my thought patterns and knows that some thoughts linger well after a conversation has ended.

This is a relational dynamic that has matured over time—as did Jesus' relationship with Martha and Mary. They were friends. Jesus had watched them, laughed with them, chatted with them, and enjoyed their company. It is easier to meet people's spoken and unspoken communication when we know them. With Jesus, his knowledge of us is thorough. It's us who need to continually grow in our knowledge of him.

The comfort expressed in their friendship is also evident in Martha's response. Bible scholar Turid Seim describes Martha's confession during this interaction as the "most fully developed confession in the Gospel of John."[62] Brant tells us that Martha is affirming the clearest understanding of what Jesus has been saying about himself. She explains why: "The use of the perfect tense and the description of what she believes is an enthymeme that can be paraphrased as 'Given that I have believed this about you, I now trust that the future will unfold as you have said.'"[63]

New Testament commentary writer William Hendriksen calls her confession "positive, heroic and comprehensive."[64] She responds, "Yes, Lord...I have always believed you are the Messiah, the Son of God, the one who has come into the world from God" (John 11:27). In fact, this confession has been compared to Peter's confession in Matthew 16:16.

Martha's first instinct was to run to Jesus, speak her heart, and then listen attentively to his response. This is a model of faith worth emulating! This is our call—one that comes directly from watching Jesus with his friends. In fact, all ministry begins here at the heart of our relationship with Jesus. That is, at the heart of what we know about Jesus.

We are called to act on what we know—not on what we don't know. People who are engaged to get married would agree that they are acting on what they know about their future spouse. Their knowledge of the other person isn't exhaustive, but

---

[62] Turid Seim, "Roles of Women in the Gospel of John," in *Aspects on the Johannine Literature*, eds. Lars Hartman and Birger Olsson (Uppsala: Almquist & Wiksell, 1986), 71.

[63] Brant, *John*, 175.

[64] William Hendriksen, *John*, New Testament Commentary (Grand Rapids: Baker Academic), 151.

they know enough to step out in faith and want to commit their life to that person. The journey of discovery to know that person better lasts over a lifetime commitment. That's what is expected in our relationship with God. We make a decision to follow him and act on the knowledge that we increasingly gain in our growing relationship with him. What that knowledge looks like will be part of our growing discernment and spiritual gift development.

I recall an example of this when my mom felt a supernatural prompting to use her gift of prayer for my benefit—although I'm well aware that she exercises her gift of prayer for me on a daily basis. This particular incident took place during a snowstorm in Ottawa when I was on my way to my parents' home. The flakes were quite heavy. Traffic was moving somewhat cautiously because the sheet of black ice under the recent layers of snow created less-than-ideal driving conditions. I suddenly found my little Chevette spinning an almost full 360 degrees across the three lanes of traffic. I recall pumping the breaks...then steering into the turn...then against the turn, all in a matter of seconds, as I remembered what I could from my driver's education classes a decade earlier. Helplessly, I watched as a large wall of cement appeared before me. I remember raising my arms and thinking, *I guess this is it!*—when suddenly, my car stopped! For no known reason, my car came to a halt, literally inches away from a concrete highway barricade. Almost in disbelief, I noticed that I had miraculously avoided the dense traffic in every direction. Not only had I not hit other vehicles, but also none of these drivers had lost control.

I remember distinctly the piercing thought in that moment: *It had to be God. Somehow, God intervened! But why would God be interested in me*—I persisted in my thoughts—*when I have expressed such little interest in him?* Evidently my theology was lacking, since God is always pursuing us!

Regardless, I resolved not to tell anyone—especially my mom—since *almost* dying is not the news with which you would normally greet your parent. Also, confronting the sequence of events honestly would have meant that I needed to deal with God— something I wasn't ready to do at that time.

When I arrived at her door, my mom in tears threw her arms around me. "What happened?" she asked.

"What do you mean?" I responded.

"A while ago, I felt compelled to go on my knees and pray for you. I had no idea what I was praying for... just that you had immediate need for prayer." Of course, her inkling coincided with the time of the incident. She didn't understand fully why she was praying but decided to act on what she knew. What she knew was by her gifting, her discernment, and her relationship with God. She was being called to prayer. That's what she acted on. And with that, a belief in God and what he could do. That's what she stepped into, or bowed down for. Of further significance, unbeknown to my mom, God's Spirit was already working in my life, and her operating on what she knew about Jesus ended up being instrumental to my understanding of the love of Jesus.

That's what Martha did. She acted on what she knew—or better yet, "who" she knew! Martha's confession centred on what's most important, that is, on the revelation of Jesus. She didn't fully grasp how Jesus would intervene, but she knew he would! Martha acted out in faith on what she knew about Jesus—not on the details of what he would do. She placed her faith on who Jesus was.

Jesus says clearly in verse 4 that the sickness Lazarus has will not end in death. He "uses sleep and waking as a common metaphor for death and resurrection."[65] Brant explains that "according to the Mishnah, after three days a corpse may have decayed so badly that it can no longer be identified with certainty."[66] She adds that four days means "he is good and dead."

This encounter with Mary and Martha leaves Jesus greatly disturbed in spirit and deeply moved. We then read, "Jesus wept" (John 11:35). Jesus cries at the loss of his friend. He feels his own loss and grieves with his two friends at the loss of their brother. To the sisters, it has broad implications. "The death of an adult brother who is head of a family is a calamity for unmarried sisters."[67]

As Jesus approaches the tomb, he is angry. Some suggest his anger is at the mourners and others at death. He maintains focus and requests that the stone be taken away. Martha observes the situation, perhaps trying to be sure that Jesus is aware of the full circumstances or possibly just expressing a quick moment of doubt. "Lord, he has been dead for four days. The smell will be terrible" (John 11:39).

Either way, Jesus reassures her. It is in this instance that what Jesus does is life-changing and life-giving for those around him. With this hope, they pull away the stone.

Then Jesus shouted, "Lazarus, come out!" And the dead man came out, his hands and feet bound in graveclothes, his face wrapped in a headcloth. Jesus told them, "Unwrap him and let him go!" (John 11:43–44)

Because of Martha's and Mary's response of faith, many of the Jews believed in Jesus (John 11:45).

Sometimes how we respond in faith affects the faith of others. Sometimes we may only have seconds to prove whether we really believe the faith that we are called to. Martha didn't have the time to agonize over her response. She seemed

[65] Brant, John, 173.

[66] Brant, John, 175. Mishnah refers to the oral Jewish law.

[67] Brant, John, 174.

to intuitively know that her only hope was in Jesus. She is a model of faithfulness in a very strategic moment. Because of her active response to Jesus, she had the wonderful privilege of ushering others to the revelation of God's power. What Martha teaches us is a faith of conviction initiated by a heart-led confession. She got into the wheelbarrow!

How is Jesus calling you deeper in your faith? Is there something in your life, whether it be a child, spouse, or friend not yet surrendered to the love of God; a new venture, whether it be a job, project, or gesture; or something that requires your personal initiative, whether it be a letter, a confrontation of truth, or some other act of faith? Is there something in your life that calls you to deeper faith? Jesus' words to Martha were pretty simple—they were a call to deeper faith. Her response allowed her to be a conduit for deeper faith in others. Her response allowed her to envelope or become the story of Jesus to others.

CHAPTER 9

MARY (SISTER OF MARTHA AND LAZARUS):
DEMONSTRATES COSTLY FOLLOWERSHIP AND PASSIONATE FAITH THROUGH HER LOVE AND DEVOTION TO JESUS
(JOHN 12:1–7)

IN A WORLD OF ENTITLEMENT AND PROSPERITY WE DON'T LIKE THE IDEA OF something being costly. If something is inconvenient or too troublesome, we usually think twice before taking it on. But throughout Christian history, there has been a cost to following Jesus. Open Doors reports that every month, 322 Christians are killed for their faith, 214 churches and Christian properties are destroyed, and 772 forms of violence are committed against Christians.[68] The year 2016 was the worst year on record for the persecution of Christians, with about 90,000 Christians killed and about 215 million Christians around the world experiencing high, very high, or extreme persecution for their faith.

People suffer for their faith not because they want to but because as they grasp the incredible love of God more deeply, they see the sacrifice as better than the alternative. When we begin to understand the incredible sacrifice that Jesus made on our behalf, when we truly understand that Jesus came as God among us for the sole purpose of making it possible to be in relationship with us from now to eternity, when we start to comprehend God's design for us to enjoy the fullness of all creation in the Creator, when we start to live in the abundance of his good gifts (John 10:10; Matt. 7:11), then we see that nothing compares to the love of God (Phil. 3:8).

Mary, the sibling of Martha and Lazarus, exemplifies what a response of love looks like. She is all in! Oblivious to other agendas, expectations, and cultural conformity,

---

[68] For the most up-to-date information, visit the Open Doors home page (www.opendoorsusa.org).

Mary gives her all to an act that becomes the model for costly servanthood—later replicated by Jesus at the Last Supper. Early theologian Ambrose wrote, "Her care for his body, the church, should move us to provide the healing oil of forgiveness not only to those enmeshed in sin but also to those who are not at peace."[69]

In an act of selflessness, devotion, and faith, Mary gives us an object lesson on costly discipleship, a vital component of becoming part of God's story.

Six days before the Passover, Jesus came to Bethany, where Lazarus lived, whom Jesus had raised from the dead. Here a dinner was given in Jesus' honor. Martha served, while Lazarus was among those reclining at the table with him. Then Mary took about a pint of pure nard, an expensive perfume; she poured it on Jesus' feet and wiped his feet with her hair. And the house was filled with the fragrance of the perfume.

But one of his disciples, Judas Iscariot, who was later to betray him, objected, "Why wasn't this perfume sold and the money given to the poor? It was worth a year's wages." He did not say this because he cared about the poor but because he was a thief; as keeper of the money bag, he used to help himself to what was put into it.

"Leave her alone," Jesus replied. "It was intended that she should save this perfume for the day of my burial." (John 12:1–7 NIV)

Usually sometime before supper, the front door would open. In that moment, either distinctive footsteps, the sound of a familiar voice, or maybe even a day-end sigh would beckon me. Dad was home! He was a highlight of my day. My little preschool feet could barely keep up with the chubby little body they carried.

With a pounding heart and arms stretched wide, slightly more exaggerated than my smile, I could leap forward with confidence that secure arms would catch me. These are the moments when excitement can't be contained, when the awe of the moment just can't be expressed by common words or actions.

Moments of such comparable awe as an adult are often God moments—when a mother first sees God's hand of design in her newborn baby; when new love culminates in a mutual expression for a lifetime commitment; when a dream or life goal is finally realized; when a heart is so full of gratitude that no response seems quite adequate—unless the response is carried with exaggerated zeal. These are God moments.

In this biblical story, Mary, a woman with a heart full of gratitude, is determined to express her thanks with actions. Her humble act is a deliberate exaggeration

[69] Joel C. Elowsky, ed., *John 11–21*, Ancient Christian Commentary on Scripture (Downers Grove: InterVarsity, 2007), 40.

of servanthood. Every detail reflects the magnitude of her intentions. Furthermore, her act of sacrifice and surrender "left a mark upon others even without her awareness."[70]

"The house was filled with the fragrance" (John 12:3). The act parallels the apostles' mission to spread the living fragrance of Jesus to others (2 Cor. 2:14–16).[71] While we have the benefit of the narrative, people in the story would have had the memorable scent. Each time they thought back to this moment, the memory of the anointing perfume would probably rush to their nostrils. Think back to Martha's description of the tomb of Lazarus and the stench of death (John 11:39); Michaels suggests that this act gives way to "the 'fragrance' of eternal life—a note of triumph soon to be qualified by intimations of another death."[72]

Some memories make a stronger impression than others. They become a turning point in life that might make enough of an impact to transform our understanding or perception of something. They might even seem pretty insignificant to those around at the time, but somehow they remain as part of our consciousness. They might give cause for reflection and maybe even transform our attitude.

I had an event like that in my early twenties. I had worked in various bars and restaurants during my university years and for a short time afterward. For the most part, I avoided friends who possessed a faith, as they often made me uncomfortable, but on this one occasion, I broke my own unwritten rule.

I confess that this man's physical presence and attractiveness were a factor—even alluring. I had first met him at a teen conference years earlier but hadn't seen him since. The conversation was engaging. The evening was unfolding well until, after being served by the waitress, he smiled at me, announced that we should give thanks, bowed his head, and began to pray—out loud!—in a public restaurant! I accepted it, with one eye very aware of my surroundings and one thought overwhelming any other distraction—Yikes! I know everyone in this place; what if someone sees me?

At the same time, I remember a calming whisper echoing through my unfounded anxiety: I want this. While it would be years before I actually came to a point of surrendering to God's gift of relationship, that moment was a turning point that helped me move closer to Jesus along my journey of faith. That moment was one of those memories that helped formulate my impression of what it would be like to walk with God authentically. What I had perceived in my friend was a boldness of faith, one that caused him very naturally to pause and worship God, regardless of his environment and who might be watching.

---

[70] Kanagaraj, "The Profiles of Women in John," 40.

[71] 2 Corinthians 2:15 states, "Our lives are a Christ-like fragrance rising up to God."

[72] Michaels, The Gospel of John, 666.

Mary paused to worship God regardless of who might be watching. Her whole being became part of her worship. As commentator Ben Witherington III informs us, even "letting down one's hair in public was considered scandalous."[73] But what is scandalous is not of immediate importance to Mary. She seeks to make her actions speak for themselves and trusts that what she is doing for an audience of one is what matters. Mary trusts that the heart of her actions will be known by God—not by the outward appearance that others are seeing in this moment. There's a story in the Old Testament that makes this point.

In 1 Samuel 16, God is directing Samuel to the one he will appoint as king over the people.

> When they arrived, Samuel saw Eliab and thought, "Surely the LORD's anointed stands here before the LORD." But the LORD said to Samuel, "Do not consider his appearance or his height, for I have rejected him. The LORD does not look at the things people look at. People look at the outward appearance, but the LORD looks at the heart." (1 Samuel 16:6–7 NIV)

Samuel's first impression was set by Eliab's good looks, since "looking" like a king seemed like a good start. It's easy for us to make assumptions based on appearance or decisions on what we think will be approved by others. Sometimes we need to live with abandonment from the expectations of others—that is, the cultural norms expected by others. Our actions of service and devotion may not always coincide with popular opinion. And probably at many points in our journey of faith, we will encounter new situations that challenge us to a deeper call on what that might look like. That's probably why Paul writes in his letter to the Romans that he has no shame about God's good news, for it is God's saving power at work (Rom. 1:16).

But, early in our faith and especially pre-faith, associating ourselves with the expectations of Jesus' followers can be daunting. When I re-embarked on my journey of faith with Jesus, after a 10-year interlude, I was very concerned about whether I could actually live the faith I had professed. I had made a decision of faith in my late teens but quickly abandoned that decision. So I was very aware of my failure. For many years during that interlude, I struggled with how I could go back to that faith and actually live it authentically. It was a pivotal moment when I began to understand that once I surrendered and took that step of faith, God's Spirit empowered me for the next steps. It was God I was following, not the expectations of others.

I refused to share my decision with anyone for the first couple of weeks, as I needed to prove to myself that it would be different than my first attempt a decade

---

[73] Ben Witherington III, *Women in the Ministry of Jesus: A Study of Jesus' Attitudes to Women and Their Roles as Reflected in His Earthly Life* (New York: Cambridge University Press, 1984), 126.

earlier. One night, I woke up in a sitting position in my bed, singing the words of a song that I had only scarcely heard before. With my arms stretched upward and my eyes wet from the tenderness of the moment, I found myself singing, "Turn your eyes upon Jesus, look full in his wonderful face, and the things of earth will grow strangely dim, in the light of his glory and grace."

Mary knew to turn her eyes upon Jesus. With humility and eloquence, she displayed her full love and devotion for him. The act of attending to one's feet was a task performed only by a lowly slave.[74] Yet Mary washed Jesus' feet, and moreover, she used a nard of potent fragrance, amplifying her extravagance. It is in fact the sacrificial extravagance that is noteworthy in this story. The perfume Mary used was foremost in the Greco-Roman world and highly valued. Her free use of the perfume on Jesus was a response of love.

I remember my six-year-old nephew discovering that his uncle at one time had a motorbike. "Wow, what would ever make you get rid of that?" he asked. His uncle explained that by selling the bike he was able to buy an engagement ring to propose marriage to his aunt. My nephew squirmed a bit at his answer and then retorted, "But—come on! We're talking about a motorbike!" My little nephew saw the significance of the sacrifice and, unlike my brother-in-law, wasn't as convinced of its necessity. The mere action of surrendering something you value to demonstrate love makes a statement.

In the story as told in the Gospel of John, Judas complained to other disciples that the perfume Mary used could have been sold for three hundred denarii. Three hundred denarii was nearly a full year's wages for a labourer! While the others rebuked Mary for her extravagance, Jesus, in his very gentle way, received her love and reprimanded the disciples.

Mary's actions are dismissed by those with the title "disciple," when in this same moment, she is in fact the one *being* the disciple. Here we see the cost of discipleship modelled.

Mary performs an act that is a distinguishing mark of the community of disciples. Just as her sister, Martha, has been the first to anticipate the full Johannine confession of faith in Jesus' identity, so now Mary, another female follower of Jesus, is the first to anticipate the full Johannine model of costly loving discipleship.[75]

Her actions reflect the breadth of what she knows in her heart—even foreshadowing the death of Christ. You see, ironically, the nard she used was often used for burial

---

[74] Leon Morris, *The Gospel According to John*, The New International Commentary on the New Testament (Grand Rapids: Wm. B. Eerdman, 1995), 551.

[75] Andrew T. Lincoln, *The Gospel According to Saint John*, Black's New Testament Commentary (London: Hendrickson Publishers, 2005), 338.

rites.[76] As Mary served Jesus in an act of abandonment, Jesus would give himself as the ultimate sacrifice for all of humanity. I appreciate Michaels' insight in helping us think this through:

What Mary's act of devotion has done is to dramatize a simple fact that both Jesus' enemies and his friends throughout the Gospel have trouble grasping— that he is going away where they cannot follow. She accomplished this without saying a word, but Jesus now says it for her. In effect, whether she knows it or not, she had given him permission to depart by demonstrating her love while he is present.[77]

Perhaps she did not fully grasp the extent of her message to all of us. She acted in faith with a fully committed heart to the love she had come to know in Jesus. What she demonstrates for us is how discipleship offers us an opportunity to be part of something so much bigger than ourselves. Our partnership with God through Jesus allows us to be tapped into a world that is inexhaustible.

I recall a visit with my aunt, who, in her eighties, said to me, "The more I live, the less I feel certain about many things." It is healthy for us to admit that we are limited in what is certain in this world—except, of course, for the foundational truth of what God reveals to us. I remember my own arrogance in my mid-teens, believing that I knew pretty well everything. Then I got to university and suddenly realized I knew nothing. Many before me have likewise come to this same revelation. John Wesley once said,

When I was young I was sure of everything; in a few years, having been mistaken a thousand times, I was not half sure of most things as I was before; at present, I am hardly sure of anything but what God has revealed to me.[78]

Mary never claims an entitlement of knowledge beyond others around her, but she is grounded in what God has revealed to her and chooses to respond emphatically and in silence.

It is her silence that speaks, contrasted to the questions and objections that are raised by some of the male disciples, and that exemplifies a servant's optimal obedience. Mary is acting not in ignorance but in faith, trusting that everything Jesus is doing is necessary to meet his earthly purpose. She chooses just to trust Jesus.

[76] Witherington III, *Women in the Ministry of Jesus*, 112.

[77] Michaels, *The Gospel of John*, 672.

[78] John Wesley, "Reply to Philosophaster," *London Magazine* (1775), 26.

Only Mary anticipates and grasps the human significance of Jesus' words, and she displays her love accordingly… she understands that he is going away… Mary loves Jesus in his mortality, pouring out her love for him today because he may not be with her tomorrow. Here, if anywhere in the Bible, genuine love is shown and defined.[79]

Without using words, Mary preaches. What she teaches is the same act of foot washing that Jesus repeats at the Last Supper to teach the disciples about servanthood. Mary's act, in quiet, humble submission, becomes the tool used by Christ to teach his disciples the importance of serving one another. Mary's actions embody what Jesus ultimately teaches about being a disciple — a follower of Jesus: it is about servanthood.

The best teachers are those who model behaviour that can be imitated. For example, books on parenting usually stress that children will pick up what we do much faster than what we say.

When I first took on a position with my denomination's national leadership team, I recall experiencing exuberance about the leaders with whom I worked. I remember sensing God saying to me that this privilege would be for a time. I sensed that I should like a sponge soak in everything I could as it was modelled before me. Much of the bishop's teaching and mentoring was without words; on many occasions his actions taught me. I learned about team building, encouragement, building people up, stretching them in their gifts, leading with integrity — especially during challenges and conflict — and giving God credit as events unfolded. A reoccurring theme was that leadership, hence discipleship, was about servanthood. It was evidently the bishop's passion because that is what he saw Jesus do. That tone of servanthood continued in his successor and gave me new ways to be stretched as a leader.

Mary foreshadows what Jesus teaches his disciples in his final days on earth. Biblical scholar Michaels makes this point about Mary:

Who but Mary had "served" Jesus in this sense anywhere in the Gospel of John? Though she is not numbered among the "disciples" in the Gospel's terminology (the disciples being all male), it is her action that defines for John what being a servant or disciple finally entails.[80]

This female disciple embraces the story of Jesus and allows it to inform who she is becoming. She demonstrates costly followership through her love, devotion to Jesus, and passionate faith.

---

[79] J. Ramsey Michaels, "John 12:1–11," *Interpretation* 43 (1989): 288.

[80] Michaels, "John 12:1–11," 289.

CHAPTER 10

WOMEN AT THE CROSS:
RESOLUTELY LOYAL AND UNWAVERING UNTIL THE END;
FIRST TO HEAR OF MISSION COMPLETION (JOHN 19:25–27)

CANADIAN BAND NICKELBACK SINGS A SONG CALLED "IF TODAY WAS YOUR LAST Day," imagining with us what that day would be like. They certainly aren't the first to ask that question, but their reminder is good for us to consider every so often. We've all heard the expression "Live like there is no tomorrow," but what that would look like may take on many different dimensions.

For Jesus, there was a finality of his chapter on earth. He fully accomplished everything that he needed to do here before his last breath. Likewise, the women at the cross got to experience that completion. They took full advantage of those closing hours. They allowed their love to be expressed with tears and commitment.

Most of us don't have the same opportunity as Jesus did to know when those closing minutes will be, so there is a message for us here. Consider Paul's words to the Corinthians: "As God's partners, we beg you not to accept this marvelous gift of God's kindness and then ignore it. For God says, 'At just the right time, I heard you. On the day of salvation, I helped you.' Indeed, the 'right time' is now. Today is the day of salvation" (2 Cor. 6:1–2).

The women understood the gift of God though the presence of Jesus and held on to it until the very end. And in doing so, they got to hear of its completion.

Standing near the cross were Jesus' mother, and his mother's sister, Mary (the wife of Clopas), and Mary Magdalene. When Jesus saw his mother standing there beside the disciple he loved, he said to her, "Dear woman, here is your son." And he said to this disciple, "Here is your mother." And from then on this disciple took her into his home. (John 19:25–27)

When I was fresh out of university as a young graduate of political science, I applied to a new agency being formed in Canada. I was enticed by the idea of being part of something new related to national and foreign intelligence. Media stereotyping certainly increased the appeal. For almost two years, I was subjected to a variety of tests, including, but not limited to, aptitude, psychological, French, analytical, and administrative. With the passing of each test I was invited to participate in the next step of the process. When finally I was offered the position, I had come to a point of realizing that when all was said and done, I had other values and priorities, so I turned down the offer.

At a certain point in life, you realize that you can recall pivotal moments when a particular decision impacted what your life looked like thereafter. We all hit crossroads where we evaluate what is important to us and what road best reflects who we are and what really matters.

I remember my mom saying often during my many single years—and to most people "many" would be an understatement—that when I met the right person I would know. I wasn't overly anxious to make that connection. In fact, I was emphatic about making the point that single people were whole people in themselves. I scoffed at the idea that in a short time I could meet someone and choose to want to be with him the rest of my life. My attention span for relationships was usually rather short. It wouldn't take long with any new acquaintance before I was impatiently trying to tolerate personality traits that would certainly cause concern in the event of a permanent merger.

When I met my husband, I found myself rephrasing the question that I had often asked myself. My previous question "Could I possibly handle whatever little quirk of the hour I was noticing for the rest of my life?" changed to "Do I want to spend the rest of my life without this person?" The simple fact was that I knew that living without him was not an option I wanted to consider. In the end, I had assessed what really mattered to me and made my decision accordingly.

The most significant observation one can make about the women at the cross is that what really mattered to them was to be with Jesus. This point is made well by biblical scholar Ben Witherington III: "In the end, it was the women, not the twelve, who stayed with Jesus to the last." At his moment of greatest suffering, Jesus was ministered to mostly by women.

Keener tells us that "women were allowed more latitude in mourning" in ancient Mediterranean society. He adds, "women were far less frequently executed than men, though there were plenty of exceptions."[81] There seems to have been four women at the cross, who were probably all relatives.[82] There is a notion, because

---

[81] Keener, *John*, 1141.

[82] Andrew J. Kostenberger, *John*, Baker Exegetical Commentary on the New Testament (Grand Rapids: Baker, 2004), 548.

of the construction of the Greek and one Talmudic passage, that friends and family would have been permitted to be with their loved ones at the time of crucifixion.[83] If that is the case, then Keener's assessment that John's Gospel is being intentional about drawing attention to the women's courage and shaming the men seems likely. He suggests that the "emphasis" would shame the male disciples, "calling for greater courage in the future," as the general perception was that women were unfit for activities that required courage.[84] John seems interested in making that point.

The faithfulness of these female disciples until the end permits them to hear Jesus' final words, "It is finished!" (John 19:30). Wright explains that these words are in fact translated from a single word in the original language. "It's the word that people would write on a bill after it had been paid. The bill is dealt with. It is finished."[85] The women had the benefit of hearing that Jesus' mission was complete, even if they were yet to fully understand what that meant. He left no stone unturned, even covering the details of his mother's ongoing care in these final moments.

Early church historian Cyril of Alexandria surmised that "Christ here wanted to confirm the commandment that is clearly emphasized in the Law: 'Honor your father and mother.'"[86] Certainly, caring for one's parents was considered part of honouring them.[87] "What we know of Jewish customs suggests that they invited a dying man, including one who was crucified, to settle the legal status of the women for whom he was responsible."[88] Kostenberger suggests that because Jesus' other siblings weren't believers, it was right to give his mom a familial bond with another believer. Because "the disciple Jesus loved" and the women remained until the end, we now know about the final acts and words of Jesus on the cross. Had we needed to rely on the other disciples, it doesn't seem likely that this part of the story would be told. Certainly, in what we read, Peter *wanted* to exhibit the same passion as these women!

In the book recorded by Luke, we are told that Jesus said to his disciples that they had stood beside him in trials, and therefore he was conferring the kingdom on them as the Father had conferred it on him. Jesus assured them of his prayers and that he knew the great temptation they would face (Luke 22:28–34). Peter, in a moment of zeal, stated his bold confession, "Lord, I am ready to go with you to prison and to death!" (Luke 22:33 NRSV).

Jesus said to this, "I tell you, Peter, the cock will not crow this day, until you have denied three times that you know me" (Luke 22:34 NRSV). The tragic turning of

[83] Kostenberger, *John*, 547.

[84] Keener, *John*, 1142.

[85] Wright, *John for Everyone*, 131.

[86] Elowsky, *John 11–21*, 319.

[87] Kostenberger, *John*, 1144. See John 19:26–27.

[88] Kostenberger, *John*, 1144.

events is outlined in Luke 22:54–62, where Peter followed at a distance and three times when asked denied knowing Jesus—then the cock crowed. At verse 62, we feel for what happened: "And he went out and wept bitterly" (NRSV). This same Peter whom Jesus called the rock on which he would build his church (Matt. 16:18) denied Jesus three times. Fortunately, Peter's story doesn't end there, and Jesus fulfilled his plan to use Peter in the founding of the Christian Church. But before the death of Jesus, Peter aspired to the kind of faithfulness demonstrated by these women. Yet he failed.

The women were steadfast! Their resolve, driven by their love for Jesus, endured until the end. Ultimately, they had a *stick-to-itiveness*. Even though their lives weren't over, they could honestly say they stayed the course until the end with Jesus—and then they got another chance at his resurrection!

For those of us who have experienced the joy of God's presence, the way God reaches the core of our being, that sense of awe when lingering in worship, the nourishment of his words, his comfort and reassurance in quiet reflection, it is our hope to say with Paul in those final breaths, "I have fought the good fight, I have finished the race, and I have remained faithful" (2 Tim. 4:7). How will this story compel you to run the race and form the story of Jesus in you?

CHAPTER 11
MARY OF BETHANY:
THE UNRELENTING LEADER
(JOHN 20:11–18)

AS WE READ ABOUT THE WOMEN IN THE GOSPEL OF JOHN WE LEARN ABOUT THEIR remarkable legacy. They are women who have left their mark on the Christian world.

Their inspiration raises the question for all of us, when all is said and done, how is it that *we* want to be remembered?

When I was in seminary I attended a four-hour silent retreat with this question to answer: "What is it that you want said on your tombstone?" I wrestled with life purpose, whom I would like to impact, what I might do to change the world, and then came up with this: "With Jesus… By Grace… Forever." I've since heard what Ruth Graham has on hers, and I think I like it even better: "End of construction— Thanks for your patience!"

What is the legacy you want to leave when you depart from this world? When your time comes to see Jesus face to face, will you be able to say without reservation, "I heard your voice calling my name, and I followed with perseverance and faith"?

Mary Magdalene could! Her tenacity for the truth impacted biblical history. What I believe she left us as her legacy is an unrelenting quest for God to show up. There is an expectation in her faith for God to come through! She is well aware that there is more to the story and is persistent even after the others have left.

My cousin Carol Ann was like that. After being diagnosed with fourth stage lung cancer, she persistently defied all of the medical opinions and lived for another decade. Her calibre of life was restricted, but it was in those years that she learned to see God's handprint everywhere and in everything. She developed spiritual eyes that sensed God's direction in praying for a fellow cancer patient in the waiting room, through small blessings like requiring lower oxygen on a given day, or even in getting through a whole conversation without coughing. She would thank me for the privilege of praying for me! When she prayed, there was an expectation that God would show up. You knew that if my cousin was praying for you, she was being relentless![89]

Mary was the first to arrive at the tomb, even before sunrise (John 20:1). Her early arrival makes us wonder whether Mary was up all night. Brant comments, "The early hour captures Mary's desolation. A woman who comes alone in darkness to such a place abandons propriety and safety in order to commemorate Jesus with her grief."[90]

She arrives at the tomb, only to find it empty. What she sees invites the testimony and witness of others close to Jesus, so she is the one to run to find Peter and the disciple Jesus loved and report to them that the body of Jesus is missing. They come with haste to confirm her story for themselves.

But then they leave. Mary stays.

Mary was standing outside the tomb crying, and as she wept, she stooped and looked in. She saw two white-robed angels, one sitting at the head and the other at the foot of the place where the body of Jesus had been lying. "Dear woman, why are you crying?" the angels asked her.

"Because they have taken away my Lord," she replied, "and I don't know where they have put him."

She turned to leave and saw someone standing there. It was Jesus, but she didn't recognize him. "Dear woman, why are you crying?" Jesus asked her. "Who are you looking for?"

She thought he was the gardener. "Sir," she said, "if you have taken him away, tell me where you have put him, and I will go and get him."

"Mary!" Jesus said.

She turned to him and cried out, "Rabboni!" (which is Hebrew for "Teacher").

"Don't cling to me," Jesus said, "for I haven't yet ascended to the Father. But go find my brothers and tell them, 'I am ascending to my Father and your Father, to my God and your God.'"

Mary Magdalene found the disciples and told them, "I have seen the Lord!" Then she gave them his message. (John 20:11–18)

---

[89] Carol Ann lived the model given in Luke 11:5–10 about persistent prayer. In this story told by Jesus, a friend is sought out for help after bedtime. Only after much persistent knocking does the friend come to the door and help the neighbour out. Jesus explains that this is what prayer is like: "And so I tell you, keep on asking, and you will receive what you ask for. Keep on seeking, and you will find. Keep on knocking, and the door will be opened to you. For everyone who asks, receives. Everyone who seeks, finds. And to everyone who knocks, the door will be opened" (Luke 11:9–10).

[90] Brant, John, 270.

It is curious that what Mary sees is very different from the linen cloths Peter and the beloved disciple see upon entering and looking into the tomb. Why did the angels only appear when Mary was again alone? Is she practicing waiting on the Lord, as the Psalms teach (Ps. 25:5, 27:4)? Is it her desire for truth to set her free by continuing to seek as advised in the Gospel of Matthew (Matt. 7:7)? Or is there a sense of enduring or suffering with Jesus by her actions as prompted in Paul's letters to Timothy (2 Tim. 2:3)? While these questions are speculative, we know by these verses that it was to Mary alone that the two angels appeared.

The angels indicate God's presence with Mary. In Scripture, the appearance of angels indicates that the presence of God is typically accompanied with a special message. Mary receives such a message, elevating her characterization in John.

Mary's lack of knowledge is evident by her response to the two angels that they have taken her Lord away and she doesn't know where they have put him (John 20:13). But her missing information doesn't limit her quest or her hope.

This is Mary's legacy. She is the one determined to find out why the body of Jesus is no longer there. Mary does not know what she will discover. It may be just confirming that the gardener has taken Jesus' body elsewhere (John 20:15), but she is persistent in questioning anyone with information. Perhaps that's why she speaks to the person she thinks is the gardener.

Her perseverance then pays off with the sound of that familiar voice that calls her by name (John 20:16)—the voice of him whom she recognizes as *Teacher*. Surely at this instant of recognition springs of joy must well up within her!

We need to note Mary's addressing Jesus as "Teacher." There is every indication that Jesus' female and male disciples spoke of him in the same way.[91] Earlier in John, Martha had told her sister privately that "the Teacher" was summoning her (John 11:28). Michaels explains that how one addresses Jesus is indicative of being his disciple, should there be any question about whether both genders were discipled by Jesus. Early Church fathers Gregory the Great and Chrysostom affirm Mary's role. Gregory the Great emphasizes that Mary demonstrated more faith than the disciples.[92]

When Mary recognizes her teacher, it is in this moment that she becomes the first to see the resurrected.

Prior to the moment of Jesus calling her by name, she does not recognize him.

Reminiscent of John 10, Jesus reveals Mary as his own, reflecting back on the good shepherd who calls his sheep by name because they know him. Jesus says, "Don't cling to me," explaining that he hasn't yet ascended to his heavenly father (John 20:17). Brant explains that there is a contrasting parallelism with "do not cling"

---

[91] Michaels, *The Gospel of John*, 634, 1000.

[92] Elowsky, *John 11–21*, 336.

and "go" that "reorients Mary's joy away from reunion to proclamation."[93] So Jesus sends Mary as his agent to tell the other disciples about his resurrection (John 20:17).

There is a sense of call and urgency in her response. An encounter with the resurrected Christ leaves her transformed and commissioned.

As with Mary, Jesus calls *me* by name. He calls *you* by name. And in calling your name, he knows you as his own. From that point of intimacy, he sends you, transformed and commissioned!

We learn from Mary how to be unrelenting in our faith as we wait on God. Isaiah 40:31 tells us, "They who wait for the LORD shall renew their strength; they shall mount up with wings like eagles; they shall run and not be weary; they shall walk and not faint" (ESV).

With confidence in what has been revealed to you, you are commissioned to share your personal revelation of the resurrected Jesus!

That's part of becoming his story. With Mary, profess to those whom he sends you to, "I have seen the risen Lord."

---

[93] Brant, *John*, 271.

SECTION TWO

TO LIVE LIKE JESUS

Those who say they live in God
should live their lives
as Jesus did.
(1 John 2:6)

CHAPTER 12
WOMEN LEAD THE WAY, ENLARGING OUR VIEW BY FOLLOWING

ON ONE OF THE STREET CORNERS LEADING UP TO OUR CHURCH, THERE IS A THREE-way stop. One Sunday morning, somewhat distracted by my lengthy mental to-do list and seeing no oncoming traffic, I rolled through the stop sign. Just as I was turning right toward my destination, I noticed a small figure about to cross the street. As I braked the car to a full halt, a man with no legs started across the intersection—walking on his hands! I have no idea where he came from that morning; nor have I seen him since. Since that instance, I have paused every time when I cross that corner, wondering if the man was an angel from God trying to get me to slow down my life.

I still see his eyes looking up at me as I almost ran him over. He was beyond my peripheral vision. I had looked in all directions. There were no bikes, no people, and no cars. Yet there was a person moving atypically across the street. It was outside my normal view, and because of that I may have missed him. My vision in that moment was too narrow. How tragic it would have been had I not taken the time to see what was directly in front of me but from a different angle. It was a lesson in how we ought to live our lives. It is God's intention that we grow deeper into his truth every day.

I remember my excitement as a fairly new Christian discovering that God's Word was inexhaustible. I could read the same passage over several times and still discover something new!

I remember asking the advice of an older couple I knew who had lived over 70 years of their lives with Jesus as leader and forgiver. Their reply still echoes clearly in my mind: "You can never exhaust who God is. Just when you think you have some stuff figured out, there's always more!"

That's the God we serve. He is greater than our minds can contain. We tend to package him and mould him to *our* image rather than allow ourselves to be transformed into *his* image. One way we might be further enlightened, as discussed in chapter 1, is to better understand culture and context.

Once, I played chauffeur to a Filipino bishop as we attended a world conference executive meeting. On the Sunday morning, I drove him about 45 minutes outside the conference setting to the church where he would be speaking. I was given the pleasure of introducing him. When he got to the pulpit he thanked me and proceeded to tell the whole congregation some of the things that he learned from our culture after driving with me. "Green," he said, "means 'go fast,' red means 'stop,' and yellow means 'go real fast!'" As the redness of my face displayed my embarrassment from his observations of my driving, he continued, "I also found myself looking for a cow all week, asking 'What does beef have to do with committee discussions?'" At that time, the expression *Where's the beef?* was popular, and I guess I must have used it periodically in the context of understanding an objection. The bishop also referred to my challenge to him to *think outside the box,* quizzing the group about the box's whereabouts.

Who knew that I was being observed so carefully or that I had a tendency to use so many colloquialisms? A Canadian probably would not have noticed. But a close observer from a different culture saw the differences. Everything that gave him his worldview (his background, environment, nationality, personality, upbringing, traditions, and education) prevented him from seeing through my lens. But, by his being observant and asking the right questions about my context, we were better able to communicate and understand each other. Context is important, especially when we take an honest look at what the Bible teaches us.

When D. L. Moody was questioned about the role that women could play in serving the church, his response was "What could they not do?"[1] It is difficult from what we have observed in the Gospel of John, and in looking at the evidence in the rest of the New Testament, not to affirm women in leadership. This is how Payne puts it:

The titles that Paul gives to the women he mentions imply leadership positions: "deacon" (Rom 16:1), "leader" (Rom 16:2), "my fellow worker in Christ Jesus" (Rom 16:3; Phil 4:3), and "apostle" (Rom 16:7). Furthermore, Paul describes them as fulfilling functions associated with church leadership: they "worked hard in the Lord" (Rom 16:6, 12) and "contended at my side in the cause of

---

[1] Patricia Gundry, *Woman Be Free* (Grand Rapids: Suitcase Books, 1977), 104.

the gospel" (Phil 4:3). Over two-thirds of the colleagues whom Paul praises for their Christian ministry in Roman 16:1–16—seven of the ten—are women. His partner Luke adds that women "prophesied" (Acts 21:9) and Priscilla "explained the way of God more accurately" (Acts 18:26).[2]

Consider again Mary of Bethany. Mary speaks only once in the Gospel (John 11). Without words, Mary teaches. By Mary's actions, Jesus introduces a radical transformation of leadership. Leadership is understood in the context of servanthood. What Mary does models humility and strength, two attributes of leadership exemplified by Jesus that seem to contradict the norm of many societies. Jesus says in Mark 10 that many who are first will be last, and those who are last will be first (Mark 10:31 NIV). Mary of Bethany is the prototype, if you will, of costly followership and faith leadership.

Martha's confession of faith is fully developed. Her words closely resemble and have been compared to Peter's confession in Matthew 16:16. It isn't just a generic confession. She says, "Yes, Lord…I have always believed you are the Messiah, the Son of God, the one who has come into the world from God" (John 11:17–27). Martha gives a powerful example of one who professes faith and then puts that faith into action. Indeed, Martha's confession and Jesus' response present a key moment of revelation in the Gospel of John.

Mary and Martha's examples are critical to redemptive history. These women have taught us something about Jesus and, more importantly, what he requires of us.

It must be significant, as Q. M. Adams suggests, that "the Lord deliberately selected the women to witness to the eleven apostles, men of a generation which habitually regarded the testimony of women as entirely unreliable."[3] His choice does not suggest that women were better for the task but rather, simply, that it was his divine appointment. Nothing elevates either sex over the other.

Wedel calls it liberation, Jesus' style. As concluded in one of Wedel's summations, Jesus liberates,

From the parchedness of existence to the joy or life, from the temporary satisfactions of the flesh to the lasting satisfaction of eternal life, from the binding legalisms of external religion to the freedom of forgiveness, from the blinding prejudice and judgementalism that narrows the church's vision to its own kind of people to an exploding and Spirit energized mission.[4]

[2] Philip B. Payne, *Man and Woman, One in Christ: An Exegetical and Theological Study of Paul's Letters* (Grand Rapids: Zondervan, 2009), 26.

[3] Adams, *Neither Male nor Female*, 160.

[4] Wedel, "John 4:5–26 (5–42)," 412.

Clear evidence shows that women were commissioned as agents of the Word, even personally by Jesus. These women were enlightened by God's truth, personally. More importantly, they demonstrated spiritual discernment that benefited the other disciples. Furthermore, the stories of these women are, in themselves, teaching tools for our insight and instruction.

The disciples, both male and female, experienced this freedom. Jesus calls—we follow. To the question posed to Moody earlier, what can God do with a culture that questions the role of women? Send Jesus.

"My sheep hear My voice, and I know them, and they follow Me" (John 10:27 NASB).

"The two disciples heard him speak, and they followed Jesus" (John 1:37 NASB).

Following Jesus allows us to embody his story more in our lives.

CHAPTER 13

WOMEN LEADING IN THE CHURCH MOVE US CLOSER TO THE FULLNESS OF GOD'S COMPLETED WORK

IN THE CASE OF WOMEN'S PLACE IN LEADERSHIP, SOCIETY HAS COME TO REALIZE the added benefit of having both genders in leadership at every level of society. What transpired in the early church is evidence of both genders being in leadership in a culture where women were not encouraged to lead.

Comparably, we live in a generation, certainly in the Western world, where gender equality is aspired to, if not assumed, although that is not the case everywhere.

Some countries even prevent women from speaking freely, let alone being given opportunities for leadership in the church or otherwise. Amnesty International explains,

Women in Saudi Arabia who protest a law against women driving face jail time. Women in Guatemala speaking out against proposed natural resource development projects face harassment and threats. Women in Iran who protest the country's proposed laws inhibiting women's sexual and reproductive rights receive lengthy jail sentences. And women in Sudan who wear pants to protest the country's laws on what clothing women can wear face time in jail. No matter what issue a woman is advocating on, sometimes simply being a woman in the public sphere can lead to harassment, threats, or arrest.[5]

[5] "8 Reasons Why We Still Need International Women's Day And What You Can Do About It!," *Human Rights Now Amnesty Canada Blog*, March 5, 2016, accessed October 13, 2016, http://www.amnesty.ca/blog/8-reasons-why-we-still-need-international-women%E2%80%99s-day-and-what-you-can-do-about-it.

Yet strong voices advocate otherwise: "Concern for gender egalitarianism is positively associated with good leadership in the great majority of societies."[6] Canadian and American values would certainly include the benefits of both genders working together.

One study by the non-profit research organization Catalyst found the following:

Fortune 500 companies with the highest representation of women board directors attained significantly higher financial performance, on average, than those with the lowest representation of women board directors, according to Catalyst's most recent report, *The Bottom Line: Corporate Performance and Women's Representation on Boards*. In addition, the report points out, on average, notably stronger-than-average performance at companies with three or more women board directors.[7]

Men and women complement one another. Within the early church, there was a developing culture where both men and women were encouraged to lead. For this culture to be created, they were countering "the presuppositions of the Greco-Roman hierarchy that were based on male priority and preeminence."[8] Westfall explains that at the beginning of time, "we were created to rule together."[9] We then "became divided in hostility," which resulted in "patterns of oppression." Most of society throughout the history of the world has not been thought to have equal societies. Webb argues that "All of the major agricultural and urban societies in the ancient world functioned with social structures that can be described as patriarchy," conceding that some nomadic remote egalitarian social systems may have existed.[10]

When Jesus came, his work began the destruction of those dividing walls. The early church lived within a worldview that embraced the work that Jesus had begun through his coming. It was one that was comprised of the "already and not yet" idea. Fee explains,

The early believers… lived between the times—that is, between the beginning of the end and the consummation of the end… Already they knew God's free and full forgiveness, but they had not yet been perfected (Phil. 3:10–14). Already

---

[6] Cornelius Grove, "Nine Highlights from the Globe Project's Findings," *Grovewell LCC*, accessed January 25, 2017, http://www.grovewell.com/wp-content/uploads/pub-GLOBE-highlights.pdf.

[7] "Companies with More Women Board Directors Experience Higher Financial Performance, According to Latest Catalyst Bottom Line Report," *Catalyst* (2007), accessed January 25, 2017, http://www.catalyst.org/media/companies-more-women-board-directors-experience-higher-financial-performance-according-latest.

[8] Westfall, *Paul and Gender*, 3, 59.

[9] Westfall, *Paul and Gender*, 3, 71.

[10] Webb, *Slaves, Women and Homosexuals*, 154.

victory over death was theirs (1 Cor. 3:22), yet they would still die (Phil. 3:20–21). Already they lived in the Spirit, yet they still lived in the world where Satan could attack (e.g., Eph. 6:10–17). Already they had been justified and faced no condemnation (Rom. 8:1), yet there was still to be future judgment (2 Cor. 5:10)... They had been conditioned by the future. They knew its benefits and lived in light of its values, but they, as we, still had to live out these benefits and values in the present world.[11]

Consider with me the following: Anyone who has bought a new car understands the tension of the already and not yet. The payment plan can be in place. Insurance might already be activated and paid for. Plates may be transferred or purchased. Yet still, the buyer may leave the dealership in his or her old car or via a kind friend's taxi service. The purchase has been made, but the car is not yet in the possession of the buyer.

In some ways, that's the tension we live in knowing Christ. His mission was complete. His work was finished. He invites us to live in the fullness of that work and revelation—yet the outworking in its fullness is yet to be completed. There is a tension between what Jesus has already completed and what is continuing to be completed as he actively works in the world through his people until the end of time.

This tension might also be reflected in how one understands God's created order. The early church in the first century believed that the work of Christ was fully functioning and alive within the faith community; they lived with an understanding of the imminent second coming of Jesus. Therefore the early church functioned with a desire to work in the realm of what God had already accomplished—the already—as much as possible.

In contrast, as the church grew in the second and third centuries, faith and practice changed. Käsemann defines early Catholicism as the "transition from earliest Christianity to the so-called ancient Church, which is completed with the disappearance of the imminent expectation."[12] In other words, the early church immediately following the time of Jesus understood that Jesus had implemented a new standard that was not just aspired to but actualized as much as possible. The ancient church was transformed from the immediacy of God's work. Kreider helps us understand the transition that took place:

In the third century a process was under way that was transforming Christian community life, making it more like the patriarchal Greco-Roman society.

[11] Gordon D. Fee and Douglas Stuart, *How to Read the Bible for All Its Worth*, 3rd ed. (Grand Rapids: Zondervan, 2003), 147.

[12] Ernest Käsemann, "Paul and Early Catholicism," in *New Testament Questions of Today* (London: SCM Press, 1969), 237.

The size of many Christian communities was growing, and the character of their worship was changing, not least their practice of the Eucharist. In many places, what was originally a real meal coupled with an act of thanksgiving was coming to be a ritual meal with token food. Clergy, always men, presided at the gatherings, and opportunities for believers (including women) to exercise spiritual gifts withered. Facing pressures that constricted their participation in worship, Christian women appealed to the example of the intrepid Thecla, the apostle and disciple of Paul whose exploits were recorded in the novelistic Acts of Paul and Thecla. In light of Thecla's precedent, they argued, surely it was right for Christian women to teach and baptize! But Tertullian, alluding to 1 Timothy 2:12, was adamant.[13]

The church conceded to allow women to prophesy, provided it was "on the fringes of the gatherings." Only 50 years later, Bishop Cyprian stated that women were to be silent in church.[14] Kreider adds that by the late fourth century women "were unequivocally under the authority of men... their evangelistic verve and compassionate caregiving, so much a part of the earlier Christians, had been stifled."[15]

It's unfortunate that the church eventually chose not to practice faith within God's preferred paradigm. God's new paradigm seemed to be practiced only as long as the early Christians anticipated Jesus' return at any moment.

Suffice it to say that what was practiced in the first centuries, as taught by Jesus and reflected in Luke and John and by Paul, was changed in the subsequent centuries. Jesus and Paul both introduced a "transformed vision of the old patriarchal schema coupled with an affirmation of women's new roles in the community of faith."[16] But what follows changed that path.

The rise of ascetics, a deficient view of human sexuality, and external and internal forces contributed to a retreating to the patriarchal structure of leadership in the church by the time of the Nicene Creed in 325. Witherington III lists seven church historians who have surveyed the period from AD 80 to 325 for further evidence on the relevance of women in the early church.[17] There is no indication of patriarchism until the second century.

The early church lived more attuned to God's intentions. As did the apostle Paul. Paul recognized cultural restrictions, working with them for a greater purpose. In

[13] Alan Kreider, *The Patient Ferment of the Early Church: The Improbable Rise of Christianity in the Roman Empire* (Grand Rapids: Baker Academic, 2016), 105–106.

[14] Kreider, *The Patient Ferment of the Early Church*, 106.

[15] Kreider, *The Patient Ferment of the Early Church*, 106.

[16] Ben Witherington III, *Women in the Earliest Churches* (Cambridge: Cambridge University Press, 1988), 212.

[17] Witherington, *Women in the Earliest Churches*, 183.

his first letter to the Corinthians, Paul writes, "I try to find common ground with everyone, doing everything I can to save some. I do everything to spread the Good News and share in its blessings" (1 Cor. 9:22–23). Paul was passionate about people coming to faith; bridging with people of other persuasions on some element of common ground made that possible. Westfall writes, "Paul was very successful at contextualization for the purposes of communication and evangelism."[18]

People still needed to live within society and participate in culture as much as possible. Unlike in some religious movements of his time, Paul's letters are instructional on how to live a transformed life—and transformational life—within the predominant culture of his day. Understanding this about Paul helps us understand some of the content of his letters much better.

Witherington III explains that Paul did not want Christianity to be perceived as revolutionary politically, economically, or socially since the movement was primarily evangelistic in nature.[19] This was key, as Christians were already being accused of being different. For example, they didn't participate in some of the activities considered normal by their society. Furthermore, in contrast to the cults of that time, they were exclusive in their faith, believing that the Lordship of Jesus couldn't be shared with other gods. "Jews alone worship the true God, and any other worship is offered to idols and demons."[20]

So, Witherington III explains, Paul encouraged early Christians to adapt to the values that they *could* affirm for the sake of the gospel. "These areas were chiefly in obedience to governing authorities and the endorsement of traditional family values."[21] But be assured that Paul's efforts in no way contradicted the initiative of Jesus or Luke. Paul's every effort reinforced God's *reformational* initiative in Jesus and how it bridged with his contemporary culture.

Paul's writings were all about moving people to a deeper understanding of God's story—and a deeper inhabiting of that story. When writing to the Philippians, Paul said that he wanted to know Jesus and the power of his resurrection but then admitted he was still on a journey in that direction (Phil. 3:10–14).

I don't mean to say that I have already achieved these things or that I have already reached perfection. But I press on to possess that perfection for which Christ Jesus first possessed me. No, dear brothers and sisters, I have not achieved it, but I focus on this one thing: Forgetting the past and looking forward to what lies ahead, I press on to reach the end of the race and receive

---

[18] Westfall, *Paul and Gender*, 11.

[19] Witherington, *Women in the Earliest Churches*, 214.

[20] Marianne Meye Thompson, *The God of the Gospel of John* (Grand Rapids: William B. Eerdmans Pub., 2001), 201.

[21] Witherington, *Women in the Earliest Churches*, 215.

the heavenly prize for which God, through Christ Jesus, is calling us. (Phil. 3:12–14)

Because Jesus had made him his own, he kept pressing on to attain it. It was already his but not yet something he had fully realized.

Our quest is to live in the fullness of God's completed work—to live in the fullness of that story.

CHAPTER 14

THE PROMINENCE OF WOMEN IN THE EARLY CHURCH

HISTORIANS HAVE LONG ASSUMED THE PROMINENCE OF WOMEN IN THE EARLY church. Christianity in its pioneering stage attracted women because it offered what other religions in society could not. Anyone could follow Jesus, regardless of status, position, or the sign of the covenant in circumcision. In Christianity, women were fully able to come alongside in faith as equal partners and be given opportunities no other system afforded. But some resisted this early momentum in Christianity, which then changed what opportunities would be offered.

Rodney Stark cites Emperor Valentinian's written order to Pope Damasus in the fourth century "requiring Christian missionaries to cease calling at the homes of pagan women."[22] Why? Because women outnumbered men as early followers of Jesus. Kreider tries to answer the question about why there were so many women attracted to Christianity by explaining that women could get into places with other women that men couldn't and that Christian women were more geographical mobile than other women.[23] Celsus also made a point of disapproval, two centuries earlier in the 180s, about the number of women becoming Christians. He "wrote with distaste that Christians formed groups that attracted the riffraff, including women."[24] Kreider explains that women were included with the dregs of society.

---

[22] Rodney Stark, *The Rise of Christianity: How the Obscure, Marginal Jesus Movement Became the Dominant Religious Force in the Western World in a Few Centuries* (Princeton: Princeton University Press, 1996), 95.

[23] Kreider, *The Patient Ferment of the Early Church*, 76, 81–86.

[24] Kreider, *The Patient Ferment of the Early Church*, 86.

The number of women in Christianity ran contrary to the population at large in these regions because men far outnumbered women in the Greco-Roman world. "Dio Cassius, writing in about 200, attributed the declining population of the empire to the extreme shortage of females."[25] Stark refers to J. C. Russell, who estimated 131 males per 100 females in the city of Rome and140 males per 100 females in Italy, Asia Minor, and North Africa. Throughout human history, 105 men were born for every 100 females.[26] Only human intervention could affect these numbers that significantly, particularly that "exposure of unwanted female infants and deformed male infants was legal, morally accepted, and widely practiced by all social classes in the Greco-Roman world."[27]

In the first and second century AD, infanticide and abortion were commonly practiced in all regions. Women had little choice in the decision because "Roman law accorded the male head of family the literal power of life and death over his house-hold, including the right to order a female in the household to abort."[28] Still today this historical reality is confirmed.

> Every once in a while, some construction project or archaeological dig exposes a pile of Roman-era infant skeletons, and the news makes medium-sized headlines around the world. But historians are never surprised. They know that it's just another human garbage dump. The babies were rubbish, thrown away because they were useless to their fathers. Most of them were girls.[29]

Methods of abortion were risky for the woman. Sometimes poison was used in the uterus or orally, but doses were determined by guesswork that could kill both mother and child. The archaic methods of removing a child from the uterus involved techniques of force in a time before antibiotics, potentially causing early death. Among the women who survived this ordeal, some became infertile. Those who were not rendered infertile through abortions might also have been sterilized through antiquated forms of contraception or medicine. This was the world in which early Christians lived.

We are seeing something similar today. Globally, countries like China, India, Armenia, Azerbaijan, and Vietnam are suspected of selecting to continue pregnancies of boy babies over girls.

---

[25] Stark, *The Rise of Christianity*, 97.

[26] Matt Rosenberg, "China's One Child Policy: One Child Policy in China Designed to Limit Population Growth," *About Education* (November 30, 2016), accessed January 25, 2017, http://geography.about.com/od/population-geography/a/onechild.htm.

[27] Stark, *The Rise of Christianity*, 97.

[28] Stark, *The Rise of Christianity*, 120.

[29] Mike Aquilina and Christopher Bailey, *Mothers of the Church: The Witness of Early Christian Women* (Hunting-ton: One Sunday Visitor, 2012),15.

In the fiction *Secret Daughter,* which exposes infanticide in India, the opening few pages recount the heart-wrenching story of Kavita, a mother giving birth to her second child in anguish—wanting the baby not to be a girl. She recalls painfully her first birth. Her exuberant joy...biting into a tree branch as her only epidural... overflowed emotions of new life...and then her husband storming into her room intoxicated. Kavita's next recollection is of the midwife trying to encourage her to sleep as *the job was already done.* The shocking account grieves our senses and breaks our hearts as the newborn is disposed of. With the birth of Kavita's second child, she has unbelievable anguish, praying to the gods that the child she is birthing will be a boy and not face the same fate. Kavita is a victim of cultural expectations and presumptions. While fiction, it seems to depict what some statistics suggest— even today in Canada.[30]

Infanticide or exposure was commonly accepted and practiced. Early theologian Ambrose described it this way:

The poor expose their children, the rich kill the fruit of their own bodies in the womb, lest their property be divided up, and they destroy their own children in the womb with murderous poisons, and before life has been passed on, it is annihilated.

In contrast, Christians at the onset valued life. Valuing all life was imbedded in Christian culture from Jewish teaching. Jewish historian Josephus writes, "the Law has commanded to raise all the children and prohibited women from aborting or destroying seed; a woman who does so shall be judged a murderess of children for she has caused a soul to be lost and the family of man to be diminished (Apion, 2:202)."[31] Not only that, but Christian women were more fertile, having not been exposed to the same obstructions to their reproductive systems. Also, Christian women in the early church married later than in other cultures. Forced marriage in some cases in the Greco-Roman world was at as young an age as 12.

In addition, not only were widows in the Christian community allowed to remain single, but their status was respected and sanctioned. This was at variance with some laws outside the faith, which fined women who were not married within two years of being widowed.[32] Of course, the right of property could be lost in the marital

---

[30] Wendy Leung, "Some Couples in Canada Practising Prenatal Sex Selection in Favour of Male Fetuses, Studies Suggest," *The Globe and Mail*, April 11, 2016, accessed February 2, 2017, http://www.theglobeandmail.com/life/ health-and-fitness/health/some-couples-in-canada-practising-prenatal-sex-selection-in-favour-of-male-fetuses- studies-show/article29583670/.

[31] Daniel Eisenberg, "Abortion," *Jewish Virtual Library*, accessed January 25, 2017, http://www.jewishvirtuallibrary. org/jsource/Judaism/abortion.html.

[32] Stark, *The Rise of Christianity*, 104.

commitment—a reason why, historians conclude, that many women of means were drawn to the early church.

No wonder the freedom offered in Christianity was welcoming.

The surplus of women in the early church caused much discussion about finding suitable mates, because many men in the community of believers were below the social status of these women of means. Therefore women found men of influence to marry, giving protection to the church, as well as causing secondary conversions, until Christianity became the dominant faith of the empire. The Syrian Didascalia "urged believing women to demonstrate religion through modesty and gentleness to their unbelieving spouse in such cases."[33] But the success of secondary conversions was limited. The fact that women were under the control of their husbands meant that they might be compromised by forced infanticide or abortion by their unbelieving husbands. It just made things more complicated.

> Around 205 AD Tertullian wrote to his wife to persuade Christian women, no doubt upper-class women, that marrying a pagan was a bad idea… Tertullian depicts a frustrated Christian woman whose husband obstructs her Christian duties.[34]

Nevertheless, women were crucial to the early church. Both genders met together for worship in the homes of many of these women. Affluent women had homes large enough to fit growing churches. Lydia, Priscilla, Phoebe, Apphia, and Nympha are mentioned as women of stature in the church (Acts 16:40; 1 Cor. 16:19; Rom. 16:1; Philem. 1:2; Col. 4:15). Phoebe was a leader who helped Paul and served as a deacon in the church (Rom. 16:1–2). A deacon was understood to have "assisted at liturgical functions and administer the benevolent and charities of the church."[35] Barbara Reid points out that Paul gives a list of greetings to various ministers, and 11 of the 30 names that Paul lists are women's, including Phoebe.[36] It was perfectly natural for Paul that a woman hold that position; thus he commended Phoebe as a deaconess to the Romans.

Interestingly, 1 Timothy 3:11 lists the criteria for women to qualify as deacons—although the KJV translators (as well as many of the contemporary versions) took liberty to change Paul's words in 1 Timothy to being addressed to *wives* of deacons. (Likewise, *their* wives *must be* reverent, not slanderers, temperate, faithful in all things). More current versions often list in the notes that "women" probably refers to

[33] Kreider, *The Patient Ferment of the Early Church*, 88.

[34] Kreider, *The Patient Ferment of the Early Church*, 88.

[35] Stark, *The Rise of Christianity*, 108.

[36] Barbara Reid, "Leading Ladies of the Early Church: Women Who Serve the Church Today Can Find Friends and Foremothers in the Working Women of Early Christianity," *U.S. Catholic* 71, no. 2 (February 2006).

deacons, but most people wouldn't think to look down at the notes. We are sceptical people with many things, like politics, but we hope that with the Bible, every effort for truth is made for ready and easy communication. As much as we can, we want to filter out our own agendas. That means that we need to pay attention to the small things that can make a big difference. Indulge me if you will while I dwell on this point.

Leonard Sweet in his book *11 Indispensable Relationships You Can't Be Without*, in a section entitled "Little Things Mean a Lot," gives another illustration of how problematic small changes can be. Sweet refers to the blessing "to go *in* peace" which in reality means RIP. Yes, you read that right—*rest in peace*. *Go in peace* is, in fact, a blessing of death! Proper translation should be "go *to* peace"! He explains, "Go *to* peace is a wresting of beauty, truth, and goodness *out* of the jaws of death!"[37] A small change can make a big difference. We need only think about what it's like to run with a small pebble in our shoe to imagine its impact.

Consider significant changes related to Phoebe and Junia. Presenting Phoebe as a female deacon in the King James translation didn't seem palatable to the 17th century mindset, so the descriptor normally translated *deacon* for males was changed to *servant*. In fact, the literal meaning of Phoebe's position as stated in Greek indicates "a woman who is set over others." Justyn Martyr used the same word for one who presides over communion.[38] In another case, translators chose to change *Junia* to *Junias* in the King James translation because church leaders were uncomfortable presenting a woman at a senior level of leadership in the church.[39] The residual effects of these small editorial changes influenced theology for hundreds of years.

In the early church, women taught. Priscilla and her husband, Aquila, were both teachers. Contrary to cultural norms in Jewish and even Christian practices, Priscilla's name comes first in four out of six biblical references.[40] The suggestion is that it could be significant to either Priscilla's higher social rank or her role in the church or both. When Priscilla and Aquila learn of Apollos' teaching in the temple, they take him aside to explain "the way of God even more accurately" (Acts 18:26).

Women were deacons in the early church. Tabitha served in capacities connected to the role of deaconess (Acts 9:36, 39). She served a particular community on an ongoing basis, providing for them materially. Her role is similar to that of the seven who were designated in Acts 6.

---

[37] Leonard Sweet, *11 Indispensable Relationships You Can't Be Without* (Colorado Springs: David C. Cook, 2008), 62.

[38] Valerie Griffiths, "Women as Leaders," in *The IVP Women's Bible Commentary*, eds. Catherine Clark Kroeger and Mary J. Evans (Downers Grove: Intervarsity Press, 2002), 644.

[39] Griffiths, "Women as Leaders," 644.

[40] Rebecca Groothuis, *Good News for Women: A Biblical Picture of Gender Equality* (Grand Rapids: Baker, 1997), 194.

So the Twelve called a meeting of all the believers. They said, "We apostles should spend our time teaching the word of God, not running a food program. And so, brothers, select seven men who are well respected and are full of the Spirit and wisdom. We will give them this responsibility." (Acts 6:2–3)

In the book of Acts, Luke mentions four unmarried daughters of the evangelist Philip who prophesied (Acts 21:9). Paul urged believers to submit to all his co-workers regardless of gender.

You know that Stephanas and his household were the first of the harvest of believers in Greece, and they are spending their lives in service to God's people. I urge you, dear brothers and sisters, to submit to them and others like them who serve with such devotion. (1 Cor. 16:15–16)

Clearly, women served in the early church equal to their male counterparts. Men and women were equally called to ministry according to their gifts, and cultural assumptions seemed to do little to limit their roles.

But with the loss of the imminent expectation of Jesus' return and, with it, the quest to live in Christ's finished work, the church transitioned. The truth of Galatians 3:28—"There is no longer Jew or Gentile, slave or free, male and female. For you are all one in Christ Jesus"—got lost in that transition. Perhaps that sense of imminence and their desire to live in the direction of the finished work of Christ also influenced how faith was manifested in the early church. Kreider explains that the early church "became known to their contemporaries as healers and exorcists."[41] The early Christians lived with "healing as a normal part of the church's life."[42] Did that imminent expectation give them a greater sense of the beginning of the end of God's work in the already and not yet?

It is also unfortunate because with that loss of expectation, it seems that the loss of the priesthood for *all* believers followed. Payne explains that the priesthood of all believers "presupposes the equality of men and women" (2 Cor. 3:12–18), adding that "the priesthood of all believers is incompatible with excluding women from the priesthood, but rather presupposes the equal standing of priestly privileges of men and women."[43]

I remember as a new Christian asking a question of a male friend—I'll call him Joe—about the concept of headship.[44] Headship refers to men being head over

---

[41] Kreider, *The Patient Ferment of the Early Church*, 111.

[42] Kreider, *The Patient Ferment of the Early Church*, 112.

[43] Philip B. Payne, *Man and Woman, One in Christ: An Exegetical and Theological Study of Paul's Letters* (Grand Rapids: Zondervan, 2009), 73.

[44] 1 Corinthians 11:3 states, "But there is one thing I want you to know: The head of every man is Christ, the head of woman is man, and the head of Christ is God."

women. His understanding was that men have a greater accountability to God because they are the head over women. "So," I remember saying to Joe, "as long as I stay single, I am accountable to God directly, but if I get married, all of a sudden I become accountable to God through my husband?" To me, it was an incentive to stay single! Why would I want to change my immediate connection with God so that I could connect only through a man?

Joe sincerely believed his account and interpretation of the Bible. Everything he had been taught supported that teaching. The traditions of Joe's community of faith held assumptions that affected their reading of the New Testament. His misunderstanding of the word *helpmate,* imported from the King James Version of the Bible in Genesis, set a tone in his reading of the first book of the Bible. Women, to Joe, were helpers to men, even though the original context depicted something completely different. For in all other contexts in the Old Testament, the Hebrew word for *helper* is used to mean one who is vital and important and even the rescuer.

Becoming one in Christ as proclaimed in Galatians is about equal partners becoming his story. The early church gave women an opportunity to serve by their gifting and commitment to the faith. As a community, they valued life and expressed a hope that became attractive to new believers. The evidence seems to show a value for women within a broader male-oriented society.

SECTION THREE

TO LEAD LIKE JESUS

Jesus called out to them,
"Come, follow me, and I will
show you how to fish for people!"
(Matt. 4:19)

CHAPTER 15
JESUS DEFINES LEADERSHIP:
LEADERSHIP THEORY DRAWS FROM JESUS

CONTEMPORARY LEADERS, THEORISTS, OR PRACTITIONERS OFTEN CAPTURE elements of Jesus' leadership. Colin Powell, a former secretary of state, in his book *It Worked for Me: In Life and Leadership* dedicates a chapter to trusting his people.[1] Carly Fiorina, a former CEO of Hewlett-Packard, as an observer of culture said, "I discovered the impact of asking a question and listening to the answer."[2] Nelson Mandela led with integrity and a promise for better. GM's CEO, Mary Barra, is known for treating people with dignity and respect, maintaining humility and a love for learning.[3] Pope Francis has been known to slip out in disguise at night to feed the homeless.[4] Janet Hagberg teaches that real power comes when we give it away and lead from our soul.[5] Max De Pree, Adam Grant, Robert K. Greenleaf, and C. William Pollard are just some of the people who have espoused the benefits of a servant-style leadership.

There is no shortage of the study of leadership. Our premise deals with leadership as demonstrated, taught, and commissioned by Jesus, even though much of leadership theory contains many of the attributes modelled by Jesus. How Jesus influenced, inspired, guided, envisioned, served, gave away power and encouraged

---

[1] Colin Powell, *It Worked for Me: In Life and Leadership* (New York: Harper, 2012).

[2] Carly Fiorina, *Tough Choices: A Memoir* (New York: Penguin Group, 2007), 9.

[3] Steven Snyder "Five Leadership Lessons from General Motors CEO, Mary Barra," *Snyder Leadership Group Blog*, January 15, 2014, accessed February 4, 2017, http://snyderleadership.com/2014/01/15/five-leadership-lessons-from-general-motors-ceo-mary-barra.

[4] "Is Pope Francis Leaving Vatican At Night To Minister To Homeless?," *The Huffington Post,* December 3, 2013, accessed February 4, 2017, http://www.huffingtonpost.com/2013/12/02/pope-francis-homeless_n_4373884.html.

[5] Janet Hagberg, *Real Power: Stages of Personal Power in Organizations* (Salem: Sheffield, 1994).

often gets captured by contemporary leaders, theorists, or practitioners. So going to the source is profitable.

The time of Jesus found in the New Testament seems like a good place to start. While aspects of the effectiveness of Jesus' leadership are promoted by different theorists, the difference for Jesus' followers is that it is about God. In fact, a love for God is what drives Christian leadership. Love is what propels leaders forward in participation with what Jesus is doing in the world. Everything Jesus did focused on God's mission here on earth. Our leadership is about first authentically walking our faith and then being available for God's love to be extended into the world through us.

At a pastors' symposium, Leonard Sweet intrigued his listeners with the following opening words: "I am not a leader—I am a follower of Jesus." He had a point.

The way leadership is interpreted by church culture needs to be challenged periodically. It seems that context affects how the language of leadership is interpreted or understood, and it varies. It varies by culture, by environment, and by the expectations that people project on a particular leader or a leader projects on himself or herself.

Often our society portrays leaders as strong, decisive, insightful, and forthcoming. So how being a leader is understood may require further probing. But we seem to comfortably use the word *leader* without much thought. In our culture, the word is so prominent that whole sections of bookstores are dedicated to publications on leadership. The cries of political parties, churches, and many organizations repeat the same theme: Where are the leaders? Despite the common and frequent usage of the word, there is not one standard model for leadership. Still, this generation conveys an urgency for more leaders. Universities have leadership programs. Work environments espouse the need for leaders over managers. Youth programs try to identify and train young leaders.

Let's examine the model of leadership that Jesus exemplified.

On the popular show on TV *Dancing With the Stars*, professional dancers train mostly famous sports figures and actors to become skilled dancers. Every week, the trainers encourage the stars to step out of their comfort zone to face new challenges.

Isn't that what Jesus did? Jesus came alongside his disciples and helped them reach a potential far beyond what they had imagined. He came alongside the women in John and allowed them to excel far beyond what culture would have dictated for them. He came alongside people of both genders and guided them to a deeper faith. He comes alongside each of us, equipping us and guiding us to grasp further, to reach deeper, to give more, to encourage easier, to care genuinely, to love authentically, to live compassionately, to serve consistently... in fact, to move us beyond our comfort zones and reach a greater potential, far beyond what we may have imagined for ourselves or others.

This is our challenge, and in meeting it, we figuratively are able to dance with the stars. Stars whose names Jesus whispers and calls as his own. Stars who need an encouraging word, an affirming smile, a soft back pat, a voice of support, a warm presence, a loving handhold, an empathetic hug, a cup of coffee, a reassuring handshake, a helping hand. As a songwriter once said about living in the potential of possibilities in the fullness of awe, "I hope you dance!" Because in doing so, I believe, we are being leaders of the Christian faith. We are being led by Jesus to lead others to deeper faith, because that is what Jesus inspires us to do. That's what Jesus did. Jesus read the culture around him, which allowed him to optimize his message.

Leadership is affected by context. In fact, neither culture nor leadership can be understood independently. Edgar Schein, a cultural interpreter, argues that "the only thing of real importance that leaders do is to create and manage culture and that the unique talent of leaders is their ability to understand and work with culture."[6] That's what measures whether a leader is effective.

It is necessary to evaluate whether church culture is derived by human tradition or God's command. Every generation will be affected by the lens of their culture. In our case, at this point in history, we may be speaking about not just a generational lens but a reading of culture that probes a possible transition of how we do church. Each generation of leaders needs to ask how the Bible is speaking to culture, not how culture dictates what the Bible *should* say. I love this quote from George Bernard Shaw: "No man ever believes that the Bible means what it says: He is always convinced that it says what *he* means." There is a twisted truth in that. We want to portray God in our image and project on him what *we* want him to say.

In the case of women's place in leadership, our generation has come to realize the added benefit of both genders at every level in our society. It seems that society has moved toward God's intention for women without necessarily looking to Jesus. But God's design, as stated in Galatians, reflects back to his intention in Genesis when he made people in his image, equally charged to reign over the earth (Gen. 1:26–28). It is us who have deterred ourselves from being fully immersed in the promise of Galatians 3:28—that "there is no longer Jew or Gentile, slave or free, male and female." We need to realize that the curse that resulted from Adam and Eve's disobedience, bringing us to a point of inequality, was lifted. Jesus changed that.

Payne tells us that this verse is so clear. It means "no more, no longer, no further."[7] He adds that the "there is" is indicative of a "change of status." He refers to earlier verses in Galatians where prison imagery is used to communicate how the law held

---

[6] Edgar H. Schein, *Organizational Culture and Leadership* (San Francisco: Jossey-Bass, 1992), 5.

[7] Payne, *Man and Woman*, 88.

prisoners, "Since the barriers of the law did severely restrict access of Gentiles and women, and to some degree of slaves, from full participation in the social life of the people of God."[8]

The early church understood and demonstrated equality more easily than in some periods of Christian history. They were challenged to live the gospel before a watching world, where their witness depended on the "integrity of the believer's lifestyle."[9] They were leaders of authenticity.

There is a story that is shared of the "games" in AD 203. In the arena, gladiators, animals, and criminals would fight to their death for the sheer entertainment of the crowds. Gladiators were expensive, but by imperial law, criminals could be sold for the express purpose of this entertainment. Six Christians are described in a public account called "The Passion of Saints Perpetua and Felicitas." They were all members of the same community and had a few weeks together in anticipation of their fate. Early theologian Origen said that Christians saw their stepping to death in an amphitheatre as an opportunity to be "in procession before the world."[10]

This particular group of martyrs was comprised of two slaves, two others of lower society, and one "well born." The sixth was their teacher or catechist. The crowds cheered and chanted as they watched the gore and blood resulting from the gladiator's sword and the animals' ravaging. But just as the final moments were coming to an end, the Christians "mustered the strength to give a final embodied witness."[11] These disparate people, women and men, slave and free, poor and advantaged, "kissed each other so that they might bring their martyrdom to completion with the kiss of peace... they exchanged the kiss of peace, embodying a love that transcended social barriers."[12]

Even in death, Christians represented what they believed Jesus died for. That witness, it is reported, brought the soldier who had taken care of the prisoners to faith. Also, some onlookers had been "jarred enough by Christians in action that they were loosened from their former ways of thinking and living."[13] Is that authenticity of faith in practice because of the work of Jesus not what we are supposed to live?

Six people of different status and gender courageously defied the status quo. Their leadership impacted the way others thought and challenged values that needed to be changed. Leadership defined and practiced by these early Christians surmounted divisions of separation deemed by society. They insisted that they were guided by a

[8] Payne, *Man and Woman*, 97.

[9] Kreider, *The Patient Ferment of the Early Church*, 44–49.

[10] Kreider, *The Patient Ferment of the Early Church*, 46.

[11] Kreider, *The Patient Ferment of the Early Church*, 48.

[12] Kreider, *The Patient Ferment of the Early Church*, 48.

[13] Kreider, *The Patient Ferment of the Early Church*, 44–49.

higher code through the guidance of God's Spirit and the model demonstrated by earlier followers.

That's why our job is to constantly go back to God's revelation in the Bible, through the guidance of the Holy Spirit, and decide whether what we practice in the church is of God or of man. What Jesus taught by his interaction with women gives us revelation for Christian leadership.

Christian leadership is without gender bias. If you are a man, you may be feeling an intentional call to more fully encourage, support, and empower the women around you. Personally, I continue to be grateful for the many male mentors who have been formative in my journey. Because I have worked more often in male-dominated environments, I have learned to disconnect gender and reap from those qualities that are befitting of leaders around me. While I am aware of discussions of the differences between how men and women lead, I am more concerned about traits, such as character, integrity, and authenticity, needed for any leader regardless of gender.

On the other hand, when I observe impressive women in leadership, I take note. I remember very much appreciating the gifts and abilities of my city mayor and deciding to send her an invitation for lunch. To my delight, she accepted! We want to mimic those attributes that align with God's intention for leadership.

Leadership should enfold the most important commandments of Jesus (which is discussed more fully in the next section). Christian leadership needs to confer with biblical inspiration; how leaders are profiled in the Bible helps us better understand leaders today. One researcher looking at African women and the women in the Gospel of John suggests that if leadership is a function of creative initiation and decisive action, both of these groups meet that criteria.[14]

I believe that in part the Christian church has been jolted into understanding the biblical origins of leadership because of mainstream leadership gurus who consider character and spirituality foundational to good leadership. As noted in the introduction of this chapter, some writers on leadership have reminded the church of biblical concepts like servant leadership.[15] Another example is the discussion on ethics, well-being, and spirituality in leadership. Ethics are discussed a bit more in the next chapter. Regarding well-being, Jesus never seemed rushed. He made time for people and for friends. He modelled a separation from the crowds to refuel (Mark 6:30–32).

Such is the case in our view of leaders now. It is understood that good leaders are expected to be interested in the well-being of themselves and others. When

---

[14] Humphrey Waweru, "Jesus and Ordinary Women in the Gospel of John: An African Perspective," *Swedish Missiological Themes* 96, no. 2, (2008): 157.

[15] For biblical references to Jesus as servant leader, see Luke 22:27; Matthew 20:28; Mark 10:45; Philippians 2:5–8; and John 13.

people invest in their own well-being they have more to offer others. Universities, organizations, and companies are now known to promote balance in leaders. People who are able to include social, family, spiritual, educational, and benevolent aspects, physical exercise, and good eating habits into their lifestyle are often considered more balanced. Of course what balance looks like is interpretative. But the idea is that people should be developed and well rounded. Well-rounded people can be expected to be authentic and whole in direction and values. Good values can significantly affect authenticity in leadership vision.

One can be sincere but sincerely wrong. For example, Robert Terry rejects Hitler as a leader because he was socially inauthentic even though he believed his own rhetoric.[16] He was sincere, but he was sincerely wrong. An authentic leader is interested in guiding people to a better future, which is what Jesus does when we seek to follow him.

God uses whatever means possible to help bring us back to those things that should already have our attention. God is always trying to communicate with us—even when we aren't listening.

The parable of the tenants (Mark 12:1–7) is a great illustration of God's relentless effort to connect with us. In the parable, servants are sent with a mission. Finally the son is sent, and still no one listens. The story is reminiscent of God loving us so much that he comes to live among us in Jesus, but still people are resistant to his message and intentions.

God's pursuit of us is also demonstrated in the story of the shepherd leaving the 99 to find 1 lost sheep (Luke 15:3–7). Likewise, in God's persistence to send a very reluctant missionary to Nineveh in order that God's love might be known (Jonah 1:1–3). Our call is to be more attentive to God's initiatives. As Paul explains, "For ever since the world was created, people have seen the earth and sky. Through everything God made, they can clearly see his invisible qualities—his eternal power and divine nature. So they have no excuse for not knowing God" (Rom. 1:20). Yet we are blinded at times by possibilities beyond our realm of understanding.

One night on a show called *Britain's Got Talent*, across the stage walked a modestly dressed middle-aged woman with humble features. In the famous YouTube clip that has now been seen by millions, the audience chuckles, showing little expectation for her performance. The camera captures eyes rolling and sceptical glances. Suddenly, she sings. She sings with a profound impact and unshakable talent that stills everyone in her presence. Susan Boyle sings "I Had a Dream"—a timeless classic from *Les Misérables*—with unanticipated range and passion. The judges and audience are astonished, and the world is reminded that people aren't necessarily gifted in the same way in which they seem to be packaged. Since that

---

[16] Robert W. Terry, *Authentic Leadership Courage in Action* (San Francisco: Jossey-Bass Inc., 1993).

first appearance in 2009, she has released seven albums and has sold over 20 million records.[17]

As Christians, we need to open our eyes to revelation that may be packaged differently than expected. We do that in relationship with God using discernment. Followers of Jesus need to be looking for what is true, even if it's not easily apparent.

Christian leadership has unique elements. A key distinction with Christian leadership is that it serves as an act of worship. Christian leadership is well defined by Patrick Lattore as "an art form of worshipping Christ, a teaching and serving process that envisions, influences, shapes, and enhances so that both leaders and followers realize God's goals for change within the community."[18] Paul's letter to the Colossians reminds us that "whatever you do or say, do it as a representative of the Lord Jesus, giving thanks through him to God the Father" (Col. 3:17). Whatever our hands find to do, whatever our appointment in life, we are to do it well (Eccl. 9:10). That's worship.

Christian leadership is thus about God. It is about who God is and what he wants to do in a particular context. When he was called by God, Moses replied, "Who am I...?" (Exo. 3:11). God immediately clarified for Moses that this call was not about him but about God as the one calling.

Christian leaders are not to be as concerned about themselves as they are about their personal, intimate relationships with God. Jesus modelled that for us in his relationship with the Father. That is not to say that leaders are not responsible for their own personal development but rather that development is one part of stewardship of those gifts that God has given to those who lead. But God is the focus. God assures leaders, as he assured Moses, that he is with them. He is with the leader to guide his people—the community—into a body of truth and grace in which humans may participate with one another in the life of the Father, the Son, and the Holy Spirit.

Living in the call of leadership, with God's promise of presence, does not translate into ease of success. The Bible is full of leaders who struggled and faced heavy challenges as they sought to follow God. There are many martyrs through history who chose to follow Christ despite the opposition they faced. (Philippians 1:29 commends to us the privilege of suffering for Christ.)

The movie Amazing Grace gives a powerful depiction of how a man's conviction to abolish slavery endured 30 years. William Wilberforce was born into a life of

[17] Stuart Macdonald, "Susan Boyle Cashing in as Her Companies Have More than £2.2 Million in the Bank," Irish Mirror (January 2, 2017), accessed January 25, 2017, http://www.msn.com/en-ca/entertainment/music/susan-boyle-cashing-in-as-her-companies-have-more-than-%c2%a322million-in-the-bank/ar-BBxQRso?li=AAg-gFp5&ocid=wispr.

[18] Patrick Lattore, quoted in Felix Orji, "The Essential Characteristics of Christian Leadership," Diocese of the West Blog, January 6, 2016, accessed February 4, 2017, http://www.dioceseofthewest.org/blog/post/the-essential-characteristics-of-christian-leadership.

privilege and wealth; then he encountered a man named Jesus. His new outlook caused him to take on the shame and guilt that Britain itself should have owned as a result of its oppression of slaves and the poor. As a parliamentarian, Wilberforce persistently and tirelessly worked against popular opinion and what was seen as against the economic self-interest of his own nation. He suffered many calamities, including threats to his life, the loss of friends, severe health challenges, slander, and other dissension. But he held his ground and helped transform popular opinion. Wilberforce had many opportunities where he might have felt defeated, but he knew the call to change a blatant wrong in society was his to lead.

Wilberforce's call was real. His call was to follow the lead of Jesus, who gave his all for God's mission. There will be tests of leadership ability, tests of character, and tests of faithfulness. One leadership theorist, Shawchuck, writes,

> The examples of testing in Scripture illustrate that the most severe tests come to those who are the most faithful...the testing is meant as a graduation to even greater faithfulness and effectiveness. It is meant as a seal of God's approval upon the work already done.[19]

Temptations and testing will come, as they did for Jesus in the desert by Satan in three different ways (Matt. 4:1–11) and when Jesus was in the garden of Gethsemane, talking to his Father before his death (Matt. 26:39). We witness in Jesus how being faithful is possible in even the most severe tests. We also witness in Jesus ministry faithfulness, effectiveness, and completion.

So much of what we know about leadership comes back to Jesus. We are grateful for leadership theorists who dissect components for us to learn on leadership, but ultimately, good leadership theory gives us only partial glimpses of the Master himself. Jesus defines leadership. As followers of Jesus, leadership is part of our story.

---

[19] Roger Heuser and Norman Shawchuck, *Leading the Congregation: Caring for Yourself While Serving the People* (Nashville: Abingdon Press, 1993), 63.

CHAPTER 16

THE LOVE OF GOD IS THE FOUNDATION OF CHRISTIAN LEADERSHIP

THE REAL TEST OF LEADERSHIP STEMS FROM LOVE. OUR LOVE FOR GOD FORMS us… transforms us… makes us part of his story. Which is what we need to grasp if we are to lead like Jesus.

Jesus modelled a type of leadership and then invited us to follow. Leadership as demonstrated, taught, and commissioned by Jesus is one that models service and invests in others but is founded in his love for his Father. In order to lead like Jesus we need to love like Jesus as rooted in the love of his Father.

A wise man once asked Jesus about the first of all commandments. Jesus answered,

> "The most important commandment is this: 'Listen, O Israel! The Lord our God is the one and only Lord. And you must love the Lord your God with all your heart, all your soul, all your mind, and all your strength.' The second is equally important: 'Love your neighbor as yourself.' No other commandment is greater than these." (Mark 12:28–31)

This wise man was astute enough to know that Jesus was the ultimate truth. After hearing Jesus, he replied with much affirmation, even reinforcement, almost paraphrasing the words of Jesus,

"Well said, Teacher. You have spoken the truth by saying that there is only one God and no other. And I know it is important to love him with all my heart and all my understanding and all my strength, and to love my neighbor as myself. This is more important than to offer all of the burnt offerings and sacrifices required in the law." (Mark 12:32–33)

This was a very significant conversation. I suggest that Jesus' close and discerning relationship with his heavenly Father is demonstrated here. Jesus seemed to recognize that this wise man was tapped into the same source as he was—his Father. That discernment and intimacy with the Father is a mark of Christian leadership.

Jesus also affirms the wise man in his understanding of human relationships. The love of God and others is a powerful bottom line Jesus sees in the man to deem him as "not far from the Kingdom of God" (Mark 12:34).

I remember asking a missionary who had spent her life in a country where women's rights were severely oppressed how she was able to be effective in that stifling an environment. Her answer humbled me. "I love the people, and I know how much God loves the people." She had made a choice to work within the cultural parameters, and her ministry flourished. Because of her decision to love as Jesus commanded, she was one among other significant partners who introduced this people to new hope and redeeming love. She was effective because of her love.

In John 15:12, Jesus says, "This is my commandment, that you love one another as I have loved you" (NRSV). Jesus is telling us that it all begins with love. When we love God and others, we will want to follow his lead; we will want to honour him in service; we will want our actions to reflect our relationship with him. He actually says as much in John 14:15: "If you love me, you will keep my commandments" (NRSV). Clearly, Jesus always refers to love as what is required before action.

Peter picks up on this command when he writes, "Above all, maintain constant love for one another, for love covers a multitude of sins" (1 Pet. 4:8 NRSV). Where we fail—and we will—God gives us hope in his command to love.

Peter's reflection was not just an afterthought attached to his letter to create a sense of prose and poetry. The act, intention, and motivation for love are not just frequent themes that gush forward with abstract and undefined familiarity. It is not simply for a campfire singalong of churchgoers reciting the words in verse about how others would know they are Christians. It is, in fact, the most important commandment that Jesus gives. The wise man knew it, and so did Peter.

As I was driving one day with my girls, I saw my running group *walking* their cool-down on the other side of the street. I pointed out the group to my four-year-old, indicating who they were. "Well, if that's your running group, Mom, why aren't they running?" It was a good question. It's a question that might be asked of Christians in many circumstances: If we are Christians, why aren't we extending love—why aren't we following the second greatest commandment that Jesus gave us? I believe that sometimes it might have something to do with us not meeting the first of all commandments.

It is difficult not to imagine that Peter is reflecting on his final discourse with the resurrected Jesus in this letter in 1 Peter when he speaks about love covering a multitude of sin. The vertical relationship with God that is consumed in love cannot but spill over into relationship with others. The fuller experience does not just benefit our own souls but it prepares us to go into the world in which we are immersed. "Walk and talk and work and laugh with your friends. But behind the scenes, keep up the life of simple prayer and inward worship."[20] A.W. Tozer gives us further insight:

> If we only practiced living in the glory of God, actually and determinedly: by meditation upon this truth, by talking it over with God often in our prayers, by recalling it to our minds frequently as we move about among men, a sense of its wondrous means will take hold of us...only then can we know a restful unity of life... faith is a continuous gaze of the heart at the Triune God.[21]

I know from my own experience that when I am faithfully spending time with God, my perspective changes. When I give God the opportunity to show me people from his eyes or situations from his angle or problems in his eternal perspective, my viewpoint is quite different. I also find that lingering in the love of Jesus and seeking God's heart fills me with the same—that is, a love that extends to those around me.

Dallas Willard, in his classic work *The Spirit of the Disciplines*, releases the reader from the drain of *trying* to live Jesus' commands. Life in the Spirit through practicing the disciplines produces followers who naturally have an outpouring of grace and a display of love toward others. When we try it in *our* own strength, he explains, "We find His commandments become overwhelmingly burdensome to us."[22]

This is where we have the advantage. As followers of Jesus, God wants us to be transformed by his love. Without Jesus we are left to our own limited resources. Most people would admit that left completely to our own resources, we are doomed for failure.

Whether virtue can be taught is a question that has been asked throughout human existence—certainly from the time of Plato. In churches, is it not true that

---

[20] Thomas R. Kelly, *A Testament of Devotion* (New York: Harper, 1941), 12.

[21] A. W. Tozer, *The Pursuit of God* (Camp Hill: Christian Publications, 1982), 84, 115–116.

[22] Dallas Willard, *The Spirit of the Disciplines: Understanding How God Changes Lives* (New York: HarperCollins, 1988), 2.

people sometimes prefer to be *informed* instead of *transformed*? Yet information is not transformational.

Professor Clifford Orwin asked the question in an article about MBA students. Replying to whether ethics can be taught, he says, "When pigs fly."[23] He finds laughable the "gurgling wave of ethics education sweeping North America business schools." In sum, he explains that we can *inform* students about ethics, but *making* them ethical is quite something else. That's because becoming more virtuous, ethical, highly moral people of integrity first starts with a love of God that transforms all other relationships.

Loving God requires time in his presence: time to listen, time to reflect, time to self-examine, time to allow God's transformational Spirit to soak into our passions, our fears, our perceptions, our strengths, our thoughts, our motivations, our longings. Doing so frees us from demanding expectations that others may have of us, and not necessarily what God wants from us. Jesus tells us that his yoke is easy and his burden is light (Matt. 11:30).

I once heard a popular Bible teacher on the radio say, "I used to be very concerned about what people thought of me and their expectations of me, being careful about not offending them." He added, "You would be amazed at how little I care now." Out of context, this comment may sound flippant, but my sense was that he was simply speaking from a lifetime of walking with God. He entrusts himself to that relationship in prayer and views people, circumstances, and situations through that insight.

In some provoking thoughts for all of us regarding prayer and meditation, writer Shawchuck indicates that leaders cannot lead where they have never been.[24] Just because people are in positions of leadership in the church or Christian community doesn't mean that they are practicing daily prayer. We may even sometimes struggle with prayer as something that we have to justify among all the other activities that demand our attention.

In a televised interview with speaker and writer Henri Nouwen, a reporter confessed to his personal weakness of being an activist, which didn't give much time for contemplative prayer. Nouwen gently corrected him by using Jesus' words to Peter about being old and feeble and being led to where you do not want to go. Spiritual maturity, he explained, happens when we give that final control to God. Final control to God can happen only when we spend time with him.

In an entertaining and engaging yet fictitious interview with the apostle Peter, a reporter delved into the same topic. Through Leighton Ford's interpretation, Peter says, "It's not about being in control so that you can do what you want. It's being

[23] Clifford Orwin, "Can We Teach Ethics? When Pigs Fly," *The Globe and Mail* (November 6, 2009).

[24] Heuser and Shawchuck, *Leading the Congregation*, 126.

the one who gives up the final control to God, just as Jesus did."[25] Transformational leadership, by Jesus' example, means giving the reins to God. As Jesus said (again interpreted by Ford), "I am sharing my life with them, and by being with me they are beginning to think and live like me."[26]

With Peter, Jesus was persistent. Three times he asked Peter whether he loved him. After the third time, Peter was hurt (John 21:15–19). But Jesus is intentional. With each reassurance, Jesus responded to Peter then, "Feed my sheep ... tend my sheep" (NRSV). Loving Jesus, following Jesus, maturing in Jesus means giving him the reins to lead. We do that by reflecting on who Jesus is, what Jesus says, what Jesus did, and how Jesus leads. So it means remembering the very important and sometimes challenging task of faithfulness in love. Jesus said, "Very truly, I tell you, when you were younger, you used to fasten your own belt and go wherever you wished. But when you grow old, you will stretch out your hands, and someone else will fasten a belt around you and take you where you do not wish to go." After this he said to Peter, "Follow me" (John 21:18–19 NRSV).

Radical love produces radical *followership*. In the fictitious interview between Jesus and Peter, Leighton Ford concludes with Peter giving three simple statements to define leadership: "Follow him. Love him. Feed his sheep."[27] Christian leadership is learning to move from self-sufficiency into full dependency on the one we are following—the object of our love.

I've been reflecting on how this concept works practically. It is a topic that is challenged in popular thought and one that is often asked in casual conversation. "If God is love, then why wouldn't I be accepted for who I am?" And the answer is clear. While we were and are who we are (imperfect, with a bent to sin), God gave himself for us. He accepts us fully for who we are right now. But people who are disheartened, disillusioned, broken-hearted, grief stricken, discouraged, defeated, or lost are thrilled to be reassured that when they face God's love, his work is transforming. God doesn't leave you in the same state where you were found. I'm overjoyed to know that each day holds new promise for me as a child of God, and daily I'm being transformed by those promises.

Yes, God accepts us for who we are, but then we are gently moved toward the abundant life to which we are called. God loves us too much to keep us wallowing in those things that harm us and distance us from grace.

Jesus first determines Peter's motives before commissioning him. It seems that knowing that he loves Jesus prepares Peter for the tasks ahead. Peter is

---

[25] Leighton Ford, *Transforming Leadership: Jesus' Way of Creating Vision, Shaping Values, and Empowering Change* (Downers Grove: InterVarsity Press, 1991), 197.

[26] Ford, *Transforming Leadership*, 77.

[27] Ford, *Transforming Leadership*, 197.

dispatched with a command from Jesus to feed his sheep only once the love issue is settled. The love of God compels us, motivates us, indwells us. We in turn extend that love to others. We give it away! God's story is about love. Indwelling that love is about becoming God's story.

CHAPTER 17
GIVING POWER AWAY IN ORDER TO FOSTER AND REALIZE VISION

IN HER BOOK *REAL POWER*, JANET HAGBERG MAKES THE CLAIM THAT THE MORE power you can give away, the better.[28] Power multiplies infinitely.

Hagberg describes six stages of personal power. The first three are more external (powerlessness, power by association, and power by achievement), and the remaining three are more internal (power by reflection, purpose, and wisdom). In the first three stages we work to gain power from others, where in the last three, we increasingly understand that power comes when we give it away. Hagberg suggests, "True leadership does not begin until the later stages, in which power can be seen as infinite and valuable insofar as it is given away."[29]

Hagberg's concept of power sounds familiar. Second Corinthians 12:9 speaks about power being made perfect in weakness. Jesus exemplified a leadership style that gave away power, building it into those around him. Jesus said, "I tell you the truth, anyone who believes in me will do the same works I have done, and even greater works, because I am going to be with the Father" (John 14:12). The offer is accessible to anyone who believes in Jesus, and the promise is pretty vast.

Jesus grants us the power to share in his kingdom. In his final commission, Jesus gives away power, recognizing that "All authority in heaven and on earth" has been given to him. Yet his invitation to make disciples offers assurance of his ongoing presence even until the end of the age (Matt. 28:18–20).

---

[28] Hagberg, *Real Power*.

[29] Hagberg, *Real Power*, x.

To Peter, Jesus also gives power. Jesus gives Peter the keys of the kingdom of heaven, informing him, "Whatever you forbid on earth will be forbidden in heaven, and whatever you permit on earth will be permitted in heaven" (Matt. 16:19).

Jesus modelled a leadership that gave power away to others.

Leading like Jesus is about sharing power.

If we want to learn from the best leader that ever lived, we, in relationship, lead from that place of love, empowering others. Proverbs 13:20 tells us to "Walk with the wise and become wise." I mentioned in my preface the professor who encouraged me toward doing a study in John and possible publishing. My professor saw in me something beyond what I saw in myself. He provided for me a window of hope in my abilities. One of the reasons he continues to stand out as a significant mentor in my life is that he believed in me for what he imagined was possible—proposing that the paper be published.

Consider the people who have been significant contributors to your development. Probably they are people who liked you, who believed in you, who saw something in you beyond what may have been immediately evident to you. The truth is that we naturally gravitate to people who genuinely like us and see beyond our perceived limitations.

When I take a mental tally of those people (besides my immediate family) who envisioned more for me, I think of my high school librarian, who recommended me for a student award and employed me to record audio books for people learning English as a second language. I think of my high school vice principal, who, while giving me a detention for being late for class, always addressed me with a sense of "I think of you as better than this." I think of the bishop who, without batting an eyelash, simply assumed that I would be capable of preaching in French, leading various committees, representing the church in different tasks, or just making things happen. I think of a friend who has the gift of encouragement and speaks of my people skills far more positively than they really are. I think of people who pushed me beyond what I believed I could do because they saw a glimpse of potential in me and chose to inspire me.

Men and women have a role to play in building up younger members to help both genders realize their potential.

In *All You Need to Know About Raising Girls*, the authors speak about finding a vision for your daughters. Their premise isn't about creating a vision for young girls but, through prayerful observation of the child's giftedness, passion and tendencies, inspiring a God-breathed vision into life. I wondered, as I read the book, how much that applies to the Christian community. We may not be as invested in the process as we would be for our own children, but we certainly have the potential for a great return.

We—all leaders—hold the possibility of helping people take hold of their calling! Janet Hagberg says that our calling always relates to what our hearts really want. But our hearts can be clouded. People usually need help discovering themselves and how they were uniquely created. God designs, moulds, and equips people with purpose and grants them the privilege of partnership with him to help people realize their full potential.

Becoming a leader like Jesus means giving away power as Jesus did. It means seeing the potential in others and inspiring vision for their greater participation in kingdom partnership. Finding that greater kingdom vision in others requires a process of prayerful discernment and observation. Becoming a leader like Jesus means inhabiting his story and how he invested in others.

CHAPTER 18

DISCERNING THE BIRTH OF NEW VISION FOR THE CHURCH:
A CAUSE TO RECOMMIT TO WOMEN IN LEADERSHIP

OVER TWO THOUSAND YEARS AGO, JESUS STARTED A MOVEMENT THAT HAS ADAPTED itself to many different languages, cultures, regions, generations, and eras. Is there a momentum to re-envision how we *do* church today? And if so, how will the full inclusion of *both* genders bring that vision to full fruition?

Circulating on Facebook in May 2013 was the story of two young men who decided to brave experiencing the pain of childbirth through active simulators, because in their words, "Women exaggerate everything." Early in the exercise one man was heard saying, with reserved control, "Oh, that was *early* labour!" Their conclusion following the experiment: "Mom, if anything that I just experienced is anywhere close to what I did to you all those years ago, I'm sorry. You're like a superhero."

No doubt, the words of Genesis 3:16 will never be the same to these two souls again. For it was after the fall—our wilful disobedience to God—that God said, "I will make your pains in childbearing very severe; with painful labor you will give birth to children" (NIV). Still, new generations keep coming, thousands of years after this pronouncement. Because when a little girl asks whether it hurts to have a baby, mothers keep saying, "Yes, but it was all worth it to have you!"

T. D. Jakes takes birth imagery more figuratively in that in everything—life, marriage, career, or education—there is sorrow before birth. He urges us to "disregard the pain and get to the promise."[30] We are each impregnated with destiny and need to bear

---

[30] T. D. Jakes, *Woman, Thou Art Loosed!* (Minneapolis: Bethany House, 1996), 77.

down with the Spirit. We feast on God's Word and dwell in his Spirit to nurture such visions that God conceives in us until the day of delivery.

In Isaiah, God asks figuratively and rhetorically as his people anticipate what he is doing, "Do I bring to the moment of birth and not give delivery?" (Isaiah 66:9 NIV). So the question we want to ask at any given time, but I think especially at this time in history, is what is God bringing to the point of birth?

When I was pregnant with my second daughter, I remember feeling the first time she kicked. I was sitting in a chair waiting for my hair to be trimmed when suddenly a little foot poked its way in my abdomen. It was an incredible sensation, but more than that, it was a moment of promise for what was still to come. Throughout the next 30 weeks there would be many defining moments, giving us a greater glimpse of the little life soon to come. The anticipation continued to build. But it wasn't until that Monday morning at 7:45 when we actually met those bright blue eyes, saw that soft-skinned little face, and heard that little voice that we fully understood the gift we were being given in this beautiful new life.

The birthing of something presents a series of indicators that point in a direction and lead to full revelation, in time. This is certainly true when we see signs of God's gifts in others as they are being developed. As we discussed earlier in the last chapter, vision for others is derived from prayerful observation of people's gifts. It is then the job of leaders to invest in others by releasing power to them—or giving power away to see those gifts fully realized. Our discernment for vision is developed first from our time in relationship listening and speaking to God and then in relationship with others.

This process of listening and speaking to God is also vital in discerning vision for God's work in the world, which leads us to the question that we asked in the opening sentence of this book. What if there *was* something new under the sun? Clearly, the question is intended to be more provocative, as the words in Ecclesiastes tell us otherwise. But what if we are participating in changes that would someday define this period as a new era? What if something new is being birthed by God?

I want to be clear to release the reader from needing to know the answer. The birthing imagery builds anticipation for something to come. The full revelation doesn't come until delivery. But let's consider the possibility that God is birthing something new in the Western church—or even the church worldwide.

What that looks like may be a swinging of the pendulum for some areas of faith that need realignment, maybe a deeper revelation of ecclesia and how God wants us to grow in Jesus together in community, or maybe a call for a deeper application of what we already know. Certainly, a recommitment to the role of women in the church should be part of it. But a growing revelation of those "indicators" will emerge from staying close to our heavenly Father.

I once worked with an assistant who was gifted with design. I would conceive of an idea and start articulating that vision. She would take hold of that budding idea and start visualizing its eventual bloom. It was a partnership that worked well. Our familiarity with each other helped. She knew me well enough to imagine possibilities with me and could even discern what I didn't want.

While any analogy has limitations, God invites us into that kind of partnership. He wants us to know him well enough that we imagine with him new possibilities. God already knows *us* intimately, but as we deepen our intimacy with him, we start seeing the possibilities for new bloom. This can become an individual quest, a corporate quest within smaller bodies of believers, or even historical movements in Christian history.

I believe that historically we may just be in the middle of a moment of destiny. It seems very feasible that we have experienced the rumblings of early labour as we anticipate what God could be birthing. I believe the historical change could even be radical, but only time will give us that revelation. If so, like in birth, there will be discomfort. There are signs that are indicative that how Jesus followers meet and grow may look different in years to come.

For one, the way we communicate has changed over the last 50 years. Nicholas Carr, who wrote *The Shallows*, explains how our brains are actually being rewired by the way we send and receive information. He explains that "scrolling or clicking through a Web document involves physical actions and sensory stimuli very different from those involved in holding and turning the pages of a book."[31] Carr's thesis is that reading books developed our brains for contemplation, reflection, and imagination. On the other hand, new technology is overstimulating our brains so that the neural paths are actually being altered. He claims that our capacity to ponder deeply is affected. Whether we agree with Carr's conclusion or not, there is no debate that technology has affected relational dynamics and communication substantially in recent years.

Another factor is the transitioning of eras. It is something that has been discussed in academic and cultural writings for four to five decades. There are many indicators that give evidence to the emergence of a new historical period. That is, we are moving or have moved from the modern era into a postmodern era. Church leaders are seeking to understand what Christianity looks like "post-Christendom." Movements such as Missio Alliance are searching for the place of the Holy Spirit. Using the theme "A Church Reimagined for a World Recreated," they are hoping to "open up spaces" and "translate the gospel" to a changing post-Christian culture.

---

[31] Nicholas Carr, *The Shallows: What the Internet Is Doing to our Brains* (New York: W.W. Norton, 2010).

Taking into account these significant cultural changes, the upcoming generations need clarity on the issues of scriptural authority, the robustness of the gospel, the incarnational nature of the Church, the importance of community, and the place of spiritual formation as discipleship. From these perspectives, we need to engage the cultural issues facing the evangelical church—including multi-cultural ministry and heterogeneous congregations, women in ministry, sexual identity, pluralism and God's concern for creation care and justice in the world.[32]

Much of the Western church has been wrestling with the changes in our society and how we should anticipate our changing role in the face of our emergence into a new era. Consequently, in the last decade, we witnessed an *emerging* movement (the emergent church) that was intended to start conversations in light of change. For people looking for purpose, meaning, and God, different styles of church blossomed to create environments that were more invitational. Brian McLaren says this of those who were drawn to these gatherings:

If they were to attend a traditional church, they would find so many obstacles in their way before they could even hear what the Christian message was. In many of these [emerging] churches, some of those obstacles are removed so they have a chance to evaluate the Christian message.[33]

Still, few of the millennial generation are being captivated by God's love through the church.

A study released in 2013 called *Hemorrhaging Faith*, a first in Canada, reported alarming findings of people between the ages of 18 and 34 leaving the church.[34] This research was inspired after the Barna group in 2006 discovered that "6 in 10 churchgoing teens become spiritually disengaged after high school."[35] "Reginald Bibby, Canada's leading sociological authority on religion, documents ongoing spiritual restlessness in both the culture and churches."[36] Clearly, church is not meeting people effectively with the wonderful news of Jesus. Having said that, the report brings some good news:

[32] "Originating Convictions," *Missio Alliance*, accessed January 31, 2017, http://www.missioalliance.org/originating-convictions.

[33] "Beyond Business-as-Usual Christianity," *Beliefnet* (May 2005), accessed January 25, 2017, http://www.beliefnet.com/faiths/christianity/2005/05/beyond-business-as-usual-christianity.aspx.

[34] James Penner et al., *Hemorrhaging Faith: Why & When Canadian Young Adults Are Leaving, Staying & Returning to the Church,* James Penner & Associates (2012), available at http://hemorrhagingfaith.com.

[35] The Barna Group, *Most Twentysomethings Put Christianity on the Shelf Following Spiritually Active Teen Years*, Barna Group (September 11, 2006), accessed February 2, 2017, https://www.barna.com/research/most-twenty-somethings-put-christianity-on-the-shelf-following-spiritually-active-teen-years/.

[36] Penner et al., *Hemorrhaging Faith*.

While there is no question that young people are leaving the institutionalized church in significant numbers, it does not mean that they have all written off the church or a faith in Jesus Christ. A good number of them still identify with Christianity.[37]

It is interesting that Linda Mercadante started her research after wanting to explore the minds of the "nones" or SBNRs (Spiritual But Not Religious), as this number "now outnumbers even the largest Protestant denominations in America."[38] In *Belief Without Borders*, Mercadante explores a growing belief system that she believes will transform the spiritual character of America.

There seems to be a sense that change is coming or happening. Perhaps *we*—the church—are undergoing a radical facelift by God's Spirit in how *to* make disciples and how to do church?

What that facelift looks like is still to be discovered. Our role is to keep our partnership with God vital, because ultimately, it is only in our passion and faithfulness to Jesus that we will meet this destiny. En route, we have and will continue to make mistakes.

Even so, some voices have accused new brands of church of deviating too far from the centrality of Jesus in order to give people God's transformational offer of hope. We need to hear those voices. Those voices need to keep speaking into new initiatives as corporately the church needs to keep seeking God's heart.

As author, speaker, and professor Leonard Sweet so eloquently wrote, "Jesus is the Singularity in which everything coheres, and without him everything falls."[39] That's why believers in underground churches in countries where Christianity is forbidden can trek up mountains and meet in dugouts, still finding meaningful fellowship—because worshipping God through the finished work of Christ is the key element for Christian community.

This is possibly how the pendulum needs to be readjusted at different points in history. We tend to lose our focus on the singularity of Jesus.

That's why the Bible urges us to keep our eyes on Jesus, author and keeper of our faith (Heb. 12:2). It is with our eyes fixed that we are moved back to that centre and may even anticipate change to something new.

This brings hope to communities of faith and Christians who, though they carry the best story ever told, can't seem to communicate that story to a world who could so meaningfully benefit from it. This brings hope to churches who feel ordinary and ineffective.

---

[37] Penner et al., *Hemorrhaging Faith*.

[38] Linda Mercadante, *Belief Without Borders: Inside the Minds of the Spiritual but not Religious* (New York: Oxford University Press, 2014), book sleeve.

[39] Leonard Sweet, personal emails, April 30, 2013. Quoted with permission.

Max Lucado writes about a very common caterpillar called Hermie who, throughout the story, experiences the angst of being ordinary. He doesn't have stripes like other caterpillars. He doesn't have spots. He just has green skin. He's just Hermie. But the unique quality about Hermie is that he talks to God every night about how he feels and what he sees. At the beginning of the story, Hermie sees a lovely butterfly and gasps, yearning to fly like that.

At the end of the tale, to his wonderful delight and surprise, Hermie is transformed into the most beautiful butterfly. But throughout, Hermie learns patience as he waits for God, continues to talk to God, and anticipates from God, until he learns that God was at work all along.

I suggest that the church is being called to be patient—but discerning—as we learn what God has been working on all along in this new season. Along that journey, we can look for those signs or birth pangs.

In the book *The Power of Habit,* Charles Duhigg tells the Rosa Parks story through a lens that might clarify this point. It was during a time in the United States when segregation laws remained in place that a well-respected, well-connected woman was jailed for refusing to give up her seat to a white person. What Duhigg points out is that in the ten years prior to this event, a number of people had been arrested for the same offence, but when Rosa took her stand, the event made history.

Could that be what the Western church is experiencing? Quite similar to birth pangs, there are indications that the Western church is being moved to a deeper understanding, possibly revelation, maybe more profound manifestation of following Jesus in a world where Jesus has become so misunderstood. Perhaps we are still waiting on the culmination of those birth pangs to be actualized into full birth. If so, some would argue that it would be consistent with the pattern of previous major shifts in Christian history.

As you may know, we are in the year of the five hundredth anniversary of Protestantism, which was a result of what we call the Reformation. Having lived in the wake of that change in history, it is hard for us to fathom that prior to the Reformation Christianity was practised and looked different from what we know—but it did.

As with the story of Rosa Parks, there were probably many events that began transforming the mood in the church before the 95 theses were posted on the university's chapel door. Martin Luther's conviction was that faith alone entitled people to God's gift of grace.

However, for 1,500 years before Martin Luther took his stand, Jesus continued to meet people and call them to follow. For 1,500 years, despite the church's flaws and sin, lives were still transformed. For 1,500 years, people grew in grace and in deep relationship with the Triune God.

So while the Western church continues to see people come to know the gift and leadership of Jesus, is it possible that God's Spirit is moving us to see and remove a log in our own eyes (Luke 6:41) in order to help us prepare for the next five hundred years of our history—should Jesus tarry? Imagine if we are living in a time of history when we get to partner with God in a new and significant way!

We listen attentively to God's Spirit and move with the groans of creation.

Phyllis Tickle has studied how the Judeo-Christian movement has re-emerged every five hundred years. Her book *The Great Emergence* is rooted in the observation that massive transitions in the church happen about every five hundred years. Phyllis Tickle shows readers that we live in such a time right now. She compares the Great Emergence to other "Greats" in the history of Christianity, including the Great Transformation (when God walked among us), the time of Gregory the Great, the Great Schism, and the Great Reformation. The year 2017 happens to be five hundred years after the Reformation. Could this be a moment of transition or realignment?

Perhaps it is like a corrective pendulum that realigns us with how best to connect our story with the story of Jesus. Church historian Mark Noll talks about "turning points" through history. One of the reasons Noll says that he looks at important turning point is to "mark an important fork in the road or signal a new stage in the outworking of Christian history." As an historian, he considers that there have been "widely diverse forms of Christianity that have been practiced" with "integrity and dependence on God's grace." He sees turning points as contextual where there were always "at least two related actions: a movement outward to reach places where Christ's name was hitherto not known and a movement inward to train hearts in learning more of Christ."[40]

With that, he highlights 14 key turning points through Christian history. However, historians have the benefit of hindsight, where vision is always clearer. While we are living it, we always see only a dim reflection in the mirror, until the day when we'll see God face to face (1 Cor. 13:12). Yet we walk in faith, knowing that we get a glimpse of something more.

Embracing Jesus here on earth now gives us only a taste of things to come. Embracing his call to friendship, responding to his leading, receiving the love that he wants to give us, actively being part of his dreams for the world, participating in his vision and his adventures, gaining the gift of his promises—all this is our gift because of Jesus.

Regardless of what God is doing at this point in history, we anticipate an even greater fullness of God dwelling among us as heaven and earth emerge (Rev. 21). I

---

[40] Mark Noll, *Turning Points: Decisive Moments in the History of Christianity*, 3rd ed. (Grand Rapids: Baker Academic, 2012), Introduction.

think that's part of what is explained in Romans 8 as "the whole creation has been groaning as in the pains of childbirth right up to the present time" (Romans 8:22 NIV). We groan inwardly with anticipation as God's Spirit propels us to his unfolding revelation of fuller experience in him. I appreciate how Leonard Sweet puts it:

> The earth awaits a body of Christians in every city who will receive Jesus utterly and completely. A body who will esteem Him above everything else giving Him His rightful place of supremacy. A body who will give themselves utterly to Christ and to one another.... A body who will stand for God's supreme interest in the earth—a dwelling place for His fullness—a spiritual Bethany. A body, who will participate inside Jesus' own relationship with His Father, and in so doing, discover that our true home is found in the love of the Father, Son, and Holy Spirit. A body where Jesus has so taken their breath away that they can no longer breathe on their own, but by the Holy Spirit—the breath of the living God. The earth eagerly awaits such.[41]

If that is to affect a new paradigm of church, then that may be the inward groaning we are moving toward. This conversation just may be building on some of the ties that will move us forward.

Again in *The Power of Habit*, author Charles Duhigg claims that "movements start because of the social habits of friendship and the strong ties between close acquaintances."[42] In other words, because Rosa Parks was so well-invested in and respected by her community, the power of friendship kicked in. He argues that it is easy for us to dismiss the call or injustice of someone where there is no emotional tie, but cross a friend, and usually it is turned to action.

Is it not true that we usually connect more deeply to the story of someone we know personally than to a face in a news report on the other side of the globe? The same is true for our relationship with God. As Sweet says, our true home is in the Trinity, where *Jesus has so taken away our breath that we need his Spirit to breathe for us*. That's relational investment—with unbelievable potential return.

If we look back at Jesus, we see there was emotional investment. He gave women privilege because of their desire to sit at his feet or to fully devote themselves to him until the end or to prompt him to perform a first miracle or be the first to be commissioned or see him resurrected. He saw in these women a commitment, discernment, and faithfulness that he didn't see in some of his closest male disciples. How important could those same gifts and qualities be to new paradigms for church

---

[41] Leonard Sweet and Frank Viola, *Jesus Manifesto: Restoring the Supremacy and Sovereignty of Jesus Christ* (Nashville: Thomas Nelson, 2010), 159.

[42] Charles Duhigg, *The Power of Habit* (New York: Random House, 2014).

and Christ followers here and now! But to be clear, women in the church have always played a part in our history.

Throughout the last 20 centuries, there have always been pockets of people who have lived the model Jesus gives with women. Ruth Tucker offers an historical account of women through the ages but recognizes that the story of women has often been distorted because, frankly, their story has most often been told by men.[43]

Janet Hassey gives an in-depth list of educational institutions and evangelical denominations at the end of the 19th century and in the early 20th century that saw gender as unimportant to gifts of preaching and teaching.[44] What was emphasized was the empowerment and work of the Holy Spirit. The same was true with many of the holiness and Methodist movements. B. T. Roberts, founder of the Free Methodist Church, for one, wrote on *Ordaining Women* in 1891. But through the years, the Free Methodist Church discovered, as did other churches who had firmly resolved the issue of women at the turn of the 20th century, that outside voices were infiltrating local churches and trying to limit the role of women. The Free Methodist Church then, in the 1990s, restated its historical stand in Canada and the USA to limit and correct those competing voices.[45] But adherents to denominations where those competing voices were still alive over the last several decades also grew uncomfortable with their institutional positions.

Well-known preacher, writer, and professor Tony Campolo, for one, saw gifts of leadership in his mom that were limited by denominational tradition. According to his account in *How I Changed My Mind about Women in Leadership*, he witnessed throughout his formative years a competent leader in his mother, who was called and gifted—but restricted. Tony's passion for a cause and even injustice that he personally witnessed formed his convictions.

Tony tells of a second formative event when he served on the faculty of sociology in the 1970s and 80s. He discovered that the church was losing some of its best and brightest because of a view that Christianity was hostile and oppressive to women. Tony's argument, which he entitles "Is Evangelicalism Sexist?," defends his position biblically with a convicting passion: "I argue that when they [leaders] tell women that they are barred from the high calling of God to preach because they are women, these have made a sexist statement that drowns out any verbal theological

[43] Tucker, "The Changing Roles of Women in Ministry," 26.

[44] Janette Hassey, "Women In Ministry A Century Ago: The 19th and 20th Centuries," in *Discovering Biblical Equality: Complementary Without Hierarchy*, eds. Ronald W. Pierce and Rebecca Merrill Groothuis (Downers Grove: IVP, 2005), 40.

[45] Study Commission on Doctrine of the North American General Conference of the Free Methodist Church, "Women in Ministry," ed. Canadian Study Commission on Doctrine, accessed January 25, 2017, https://fmcic.ca/women-in-ministry-fmcna-fmcic/.

tap dancing they may do when making their assertions."[46] Strong personal ties led Tony's convictions with a fire in his belly, which Duhigg claims is necessary for any movement.

Perhaps the last 50 years have already been part of the rumblings to a new movement. Certainly, we needed to put to rest any question about whether one gender is chosen over the other in leadership.

Other leaders have drawn similar conclusions. Bill Hybels states his position from a premise of necessity in the early days of planting Willow Creek:

> In actual experience, it was easier to find high school girls who were spiritually mature and skilled in leadership than it was to find guys. From a practical standpoint, it would have been unthinkable not to allow girls to lead.[47]

Were these revelations contributing to a pendulum swing that is still happening and should have existed all along—and in some ways did? Because throughout church history, women have assumed roles as evangelists, teachers, missionaries, pioneers, martyrs, and church leaders at the onset of movements—especially in the early church.

As an example, going back to the fourth century Rome, Ruth Tucker cites Marcella as an early pioneer who "was also known for her keen mind and understanding of the Bible." Closely working with Jerome (Vulgate Bible translator), she was the one Jerome referred others to in his absence. "'If an argument arose about some evidence from Scripture,' he wrote, 'the question was pursued with her as the judge.'"[48] There seemed to be a respectful partnership by gifting.

God's calling of both genders to partner with him in his mission was always God's intention—even in the fog of culture.

Still, the Roman Catholic Church insists that women are not to be clergy because the apostles were men. Pope Francis has been asked on two recorded occasions whether there is any intention to change the traditional stand, and he has as recently as November 2016 said, "No." This, despite a glimmer of hope that had been ignited in August of 2016 when the pope agreed to appointing a committee to look at women in the early church.[49]

---

[46] Tony Campolo, "Is Evangelicalism Sexist?," in *How I Changed My Mind About Women in Leadership: Compelling Stories from Prominent Evangelicals*, ed. Alan F. Johnson (Grand Rapids: Zondervan, 2010), 69.

[47] Bill Hybels and Lynne Hybels, "Evangelicals and Gender Equality," in *How I Changed My Mind About Women in Leadership: Compelling Stories from Prominent Evangelicals*, ed. Alan F. Johnson (Grand Rapids: Zondervan, 2010), 107.

[48] Tucker, "The Changing Roles of Women in Ministry," 26.

[49] Philip Pullella, "Pope Orders Study of Women's Role in Early Church, Cheering Equality Campaigners," *Reuters* (August 2, 2016), accessed January 25, 2017, http://www.reuters.com/article/us-pope-women-idUSKCN10D-1AB.

To the female reporter, he said, "St. Pope John Paul II had the last clear word on this and it stands, this stands." The reporter retorted, "But forever, forever? Never, never?"

Pope Francis answered, "If we read carefully the declaration by St. John Paul II, it is going in that direction."[50] The Apostolic Letter by John Paul II, On Reserving Priestly Ordination to Men Alone, begins as follows:

Priestly ordination, which hands on the office entrusted by Christ to his Apostles of teaching, sanctifying and governing the faithful, has in the Catholic Church from the beginning always been reserved to men alone. This tradition has also been faithfully maintained by the Oriental Churches.[51]

In this same document, John Paul II defended his position, referring back to Pope Paul VI's statement from the time when the Anglican Communion reconsidered their position on women:

[The Catholic Church] holds that it is not admissible to ordain women to the priesthood, for very fundamental reasons. These reasons include: the example recorded in the Sacred Scriptures of Christ choosing his Apostles only from among men; the constant practice of the Church, which has imitated Christ in choosing only men; and her living teaching authority which has consistently held that the exclusion of women from the priesthood is in accordance with God's plan for his Church.[52]

Other churches have isolated verses out of context as their reason for women not to be ordained, usually echoing that roles are different.

I remember hearing a fellow seminarian similarly proclaiming that women's roles are clearly defined by the fact that the disciples are all men. It was recently brought to my attention that the disciples were also all assumed to be under the age of 20, except for Peter. Does that mean that all leaders in the church should be under the age of 30?

In a David-Letterman-style list, Fuller professor Dr. Scholer in his class Women and the Bible and the Church argued tongue-in-cheek using much of the common

[50] Philip Pullella, "Pope Says He Believes Ban on Female Priests Is Forever," *Reuters* (November 1, 2016), accessed January 25, 2017, http://www.reuters.com/article/us-pope-women-idUSKBN12W4L7.

[51] John Paul II, "Apostolic Letter *Odinatio Sacerdotalis* of John Paul II to the Bishops of the Catholic Church On Reserving Priestly Ordination to Men Alone," *Apostolic Letters* (Vatican: Libreria Editrice Vaticana, 1994), accessed January 25, 2017, https://w2.vatican.va/content/john-paul-ii/en/apost_letters/1994/documents/hf_jp-ii_apl_19940522_ordinatio-sacerdotalis.html.

[52] Paul II, "Apostolic Letter *Odinatio Sacerdotalis*."

reasoning for women to have been refused ordination or positions of leadership in the church. It is intended to be not offensive but rather just witty, giving cause for reflection. Please see it from that lens.

TOP TEN REASONS WHY MEN SHOULD NOT BE ORDAINED[53]

10. A man's place is in the army.

9. For men who have children, their duties might distract them from the responsibilities of being a parent.

8. Their physical build indicates that men are more suited to tasks such as chopping down trees and wrestling mountain lions. It would be "unnatural" for them to do other forms of work.

7. Man was created before woman. It is therefore obvious that man was a prototype. Thus, they represent an experiment, rather than the crowning achievement of creation.

6. Men are too emotional to be priests or pastors. This is easily demonstrated by their conduct at football games and watching basketball tournaments.

5. Some men are handsome; they will distract women worshipers.

4. To be [an] ordained pastor is to nurture the congregation. But this is not a traditional male role. Rather, throughout history, women have been considered to be not only more skilled than men at nurturing, but also more frequently attracted to it. This makes them the obvious choice for ordination.

3. Men are overly prone to violence. No really manly man wants to settle disputes by any means other than by fighting about it. Thus, they would be poor role models, as well as being dangerously unstable in positions of leadership.

2. Men can still be involved in church activities, even without being ordained. They can sweep paths, repair the church roof, and maybe even lead the singing on Father's Day. By confining themselves to such traditional male roles, they can still be vitally important in the life of the Church.

1. In the New Testament account, the person who betrayed Jesus was a man. Thus, his lack of faith and ensuing punishment stands as a symbol of the subordinated position that all men should take.

It isn't uncommon for students of the Bible to change their convictions once faced with God's interaction with women in the Bible as a whole. *How I Changed My Mind About Women in Leadership* includes stories from various Christians leaders who changed their convictions about God's call to women.

---

[53] Original source is unknown. This list was adapted to the current list by the late Dr. David M. Scholer, a former professor at Fuller Theological Seminary.

Another example is Dr. Gilbert Bilezikian of Wheaton College, also a member of Willow Creek where Bill Hybels pastored, who authored a book as a result of Willow Creek's quest for biblical fidelity. He concluded that, before the fall, both genders were created equal in God's image to participate in the care of the world. In Jesus, as we read in Ephesians 2:22, we are all being built together to become a dwelling in which God lives. What God created before the fall is our ongoing quest. Our "being built together" is a journey of spiritual growth or sanctification, if you will, that leads us back to God's intended design for us.

Rebecca Groothuis writes, "Regardless of how hierarchalists try to explain the situation, the idea that women are equal *in* their being, yet unequal *by virtue of* their being, is contradictory and ultimately nonsensical."[54] *How I Changed My Mind about Women in Leadership* presents each case as a personal account where different leaders allowed the story of Jesus to live through their real-life experiences. In the foreword, Dallas Willard recognizes how the gender issue is neither "marginal" nor "minor." He writes, "It profoundly affects the sense of identity and worth on both sides of the gender line; and, if wrongly grasped, it restricts the resources for blessing, through the church, upon an appallingly needy world."[55]

If we are in a time of transition and revelation, then we want to discourage all obstacles that would otherwise stand in the way. Why would we want to "restrict the resources of blessing," in the words of Willard? Rather, we want to instill a sense of identity and worth in both genders that leads us to the full potential of Christ's church. As followers of Jesus, we can own our story in Christ. As with faith, until you make the story your own—when you allow the fabric of God's Spirit to weave new life into the old wineskin; when you experience how to live in community with the triune God; when you live truth in the person of Jesus along a journey that grows in grace—you just won't get it. So it may be true for many with God's indiscriminate call to women.

Perhaps we need to repeatedly ask what is being communicated by our actions, behaviours, and words. Those will stem from what we believe. If we believe that God's story is a grand narrative with many sub-narratives—as I believe it is—and we know that God is the same yesterday, today, and tomorrow (Mal. 3:6; Heb. 13:8), then we need to always test our conclusions. I believe that God has clear eternal principles and intentions for women in leadership and ordination.

To any *unchurched* readers who may be exploring Jesus, some of this discussion may be as much of a cultural shock to you as the show *Mad Men*—a television show that depicts life as it was in the 1960s. Even if you have been raised outside of a

---

[54] Groothuis, *Good News for Women*, 55. Hierarchicalists claim that there is an eternal subordination in God that is replicated in created order.

[55] Dallas Willard, foreword to *How I Changed My Mind About Women in Leadership: Compelling Stories from Prominent Evangelicals*, ed. Alan F. Johnson (Grand Rapids: Zondervan, 2010), 11.

faith tradition with a strong sense of equality, some faith traditions can confuse you on your spiritual journey into believing practices that were never within God's plan but are suddenly expected of you as part of that church culture. Or maybe you were raised in a faith tradition and have sensed a call beyond the borders of your culture and are trying to wrestle with what that looks like.

Hopefully this book helps us unmask unfounded assumptions. Because I believe that we live in a season that requires all hands on deck!

God's story will hold its own.

Your role is to become that story.

CHAPTER 19

LEADERS FOLLOW JESUS, THEN INVEST IN THE MAKING OF OTHER LEADERS

JESUS SAID, "FOLLOW ME, AND I WILL MAKE YOU FISHERS OF MEN" (MATT. 4:19 ESV). The ability to fish was never something that was expected to be mastered without the benefit of transformational change. Leighton Ford picks up on this promise as a hope for aspiring leaders. The promise is clear that leaders are developed—not born. Kouzes and Posner claim that people are far more capable of developing themselves as leaders than tradition has ever assumed possible. God claims to have called the weak in the world—not the powerful and not necessarily the wise (1 Cor. 1:27). God is the source of their—our—strength. It is God who makes us fishers of men.

Leadership is a journey—a process that puts God at the centre and trusts in his faithfulness. It is a process that prompts leaders to engage in love relationships that deepen through surrender and dependency on a sovereign God. It is a relationship that puts others first and sees their potential through the eyes of God. It is a relationship that sees itself as having the privilege of partnering with the living God in an unfolding story in which he is already at work. Leadership is about God moving in his people.

Leaders gifted with courageous patience will discern vision. Vision will develop not from leaders but in their active, living relationships with God and the community. The anticipation assumes that God is already at work, taking people along in the journey. Leadership author Lovett Weems illustrates the excitement of the journey of vision by referring to the "Gretzky Factor."[56] Wayne Gretzky is admired as the best

---

[56] Lovett H. Weems Jr., *Church Leadership: Vision, Team, Culture and Integrity* (Nashville: Abingdon Press, 1993), 60.

hockey player of his generation. Weem's wise words are insightful for leadership. Gretzky knew that what mattered wasn't where the puck was at any given moment but where the puck was going. That's the quest for a leader—to discern where the next step is going—to discerning how vision will be unfolding.

One leadership analogy is that of a mother cradling a child in her arms and then nurturing the child's gifts, promise, and passions. The image encourages us to discern and nurture God's vision for the child. A mother's instinct is to put herself aside and invest herself into the raising of that child.

At the dedication of my firstborn, her aunt sang a memorable song. The tribute envisioned the child's potential, but the chorus returned us to the beautiful cradled infant, so dependent and so full of life and promise—"but, I'm sure going to miss who you are." A mother loves the current reality, lives to enjoy every moment of the journey, but keeps focused on her desire to see that baby achieve all of her promise.

Leaders see the beauty and promise in the people whom they lead yet love them just as they are. The investment of care and nurturing is not for the sake of arriving at an end product but about guiding the process of transformation in people's lives.

Leaders help others grow in the story of Jesus.

CHAPTER 20

LEARNING FROM JESUS, LIVING LIKE JESUS, LEADING LIKE JESUS:
BECOMING THE BEST STORY EVER

I BOUGHT A PAINTING FROM A LOCAL STREET ARTIST IN QUEBEC. THE PAINTING depicts a mother and child. The mother's arms are almost disproportional to the rest of her body. Her child appears fully at rest in the strength and security of his mother's embrace. Many times through that night, I reflected on the painting, the restful facial expressions, the mother's strong grip of reassurance, the child's security of knowing there is nowhere he'd rather be, the love of parent and child. Something about the picture created an image of invitation.

Jesus invites us to be fully embraced by the Father. Jesus disregarded cultural impediments of his day and called men and women equally into full partnership. That partnership grows as our relationship with God deepens.

In Matthew 25, Jesus tells a parable about the distribution of talents. The story is told of a man who leaves for a journey, entrusting five talents to one servant, two to another, and one talent to the third. The two servants with multiple talents return an even greater amount when the master returns and are greeted with the words "Well done, my good and faithful servant" (Matt. 25:21, 23). Furthermore, they are put in charge of many things and are invited to share in the master's joy. The third servant expresses his fear in having not taken risks and confesses to having hidden his talent in the ground. He returns to the master only what was entrusted to him with no interest, no further investment, no increased value, no creative use for further development. The master's words are harsh and sobering. The servant is called lazy and wicked for not being wise with the talent distributed by the master. Even what the last servant was given is taken away and reassigned to the servants whose investment showed return. In fact, the first two servants were entrusted with even more, as they had proven themselves worthy.

When all is said and done, on the day the Son of Man comes in glory (Matt. 25:31), what are the words that will inspire you to deeper partnership? Are there gifts and talents you are hiding in the ground? Are you responding to the call of Jesus—fully embraced in that security? That's the hope of God's promise.

What's more is our time in history, which is enabling us to reassess some of our assumptions and anticipate a new birth in how the church functions in our world. While we await its full revelation as we would a new baby, many would concur that God *is* doing something new. This *something new* encourages us to reconnect with God's intention for the church and how the earliest church lived that. Traditions and practices that seem out of line to that intention need to be questioned.

Strip away those things that impede God's call, whether they are man-made rules, culture, or avoidance. Look instead to those things that provide us with a host of references for our further engagement in God's purposes. We endure with perseverance because we have a hope that inspires us to greater things.

> Therefore, since we are surrounded by such a huge crowd of witnesses to the life of faith, let us strip off every weight that slows us down, especially the sin that so easily trips us up. And let us run with endurance the race God has set before us. We do this by keeping our eyes on Jesus, the champion who initiates and perfects our faith. (Hebrews 12:1–2)

Go now *to* peace—be blessed forward! Receive your blessing for life, understanding it as a "wresting of beauty, truth, and goodness out of the jaws of death, and a push to make the best use of whatever life remains," a blessing with energies that produces "wholeness and wellness to the world."[57]

Listen to Jesus.
Learn from Jesus.
Lead like Jesus.
Go and become the best story ever told!
Go and become his story!

---

[57] Leonard, *11 Indispensable Relationships*, 62–63.

OTHER BOOKS BY

CASTLE QUAY BOOKS

Faith, Life & Leadership

8 CANADIAN WOMEN TELL THEIR STORIES

General Editor, Georgialee Lang

FOREWORD BY DR BRIAN STILLER

Global Ambassador, World Evangelical Alliance

WHO AM I?

a devotional journey for you to soar in your identity in Christ

SHARON SIMMONDS

Foreword by Steve A. Brown

"Imagine a treasure box for leaders with everything you could possibly need in it..."

from the foreword by Mark Buchanan

Leading Me

Eight Practices for a Christian Leader's
Most Important Assignment

Steve A. Brown

because God was there

A JOURNEY OF LOSS, HEALING AND OVERCOMING

BELMA VARDY